DATE DUE		

THE HISTORY OF WEAPONS AND WARFARE

THE MIDDLE AGES

THE MIDDLE AGES

Other books in this series include:

Ancient Egypt
Ancient Greece
Ancient Rome
The Civil War
The Native Americans

THE MIDDLE AGES

BY DON NARDO

LUCENT
BOOKS ®

THOMSON
—————★—————™
GALE

San Diego • Detroit • New York • San Francisco • Cleveland • New Haven, Conn. • Waterville, Maine • London • Munich

On Cover: The victory of Heraclius over the Sassanian.

LIBRARY OF CONGRESS CATALOGING-IN-PUBLICATION DATA

Nardo, Don, 1947–
   The Middle Ages / by Don Nardo.
      p. cm. — (The history of weapons and warfare)
Summary: Discusses the weapons, tactics, gunpowder, castles, fortifications, cannons, handheld guns, ships and other weapons used in the Middle Ages warfare.
Includes bibliographical references and index.
   ISBN 1-59018-069-0
   1. Military art and science—Europe—History, Medieval–500–1500—Juvenile literature. 2. Civilization, Medieval—Juvenile literature. 3. Knights and knighthood—Juvenile literature. 4. Castles—Juvenile literature. I. Title. II. Series.
   U37.N37 2003
   355'.0094'0902—dc21

                                                              2002006253

Contents

Foreword

The earliest battle about which any detailed information has survived took place in 1274 B.C. at Kadesh, in Syria, when the armies of the Egyptian and Hittite empires clashed. For this reason, modern historians devote a good deal of attention to Kadesh. They know that this battle and the war of which it was a part were not the first fought by the Egyptians and their neighbors. Many other earlier conflicts are mentioned in ancient inscriptions found throughout the Near East and other regions, as from the dawn of recorded history city-states fought one another for political or economic dominance.

Moreover, it is likely that warfare long predated city-states and written records. Some scholars go so far as to suggest that the Cro-Magnons, the direct ancestors of modern humans, wiped out another early human group—the Neanderthals—in a prolonged and fateful conflict in the dim past. Even if this did not happen, it is likely that even the earliest humans engaged in conflicts and battles over territory and other factors. "Warfare is almost as old as man himself," writes renowned military historian John Keegan, "and reaches into the most secret places of the human heart, places where self dissolves rational purpose, where pride reigns, where emotion is paramount, where instinct is king."

Even after humans became "civilized," with cities, writing, and organized religion, the necessity of war was widely accepted. Most people saw it as the most natural means of defending territory, maintaining security, or settling disputes. A character in a dialogue by the fourth-century B.C. Greek thinker Plato declares:

> All men are always at war with one another. . . . For what men in general term peace is only a name; in reality, every city is in a natural state of war with every other, not indeed proclaimed by heralds, but everlasting. . . . No possessions or institutions are of any value to him who is defeated in battle; for all the good things of the conquered pass into the hands of the conquerors.

Considering the thousands of conflicts that have raged across the world since Plato's time, it would seem that war is an inevitable part of the human condition.

War not only remains an ever-present reality, it has also had undeniably crucial and far-reaching effects on human society and its development. As Keegan puts it, "History lessons remind us that the states in which we live . . . have come to us through conflict, often of the most bloodthirsty sort." Indeed, the world's first and oldest nation-state,

Egypt, was born out of a war between the two kingdoms that originally occupied the area; the modern nations of Europe rose from the wreckage of the sweeping barbarian invasions that destroyed the Roman Empire; and the United States was established by a bloody revolution between British colonists and their mother country.

Victory in these and other wars resulted from varying factors. Sometimes the side that possessed overwhelming numbers or the most persistence won; other times superior generalship and strategy played key roles. In many cases, the side with the most advanced and deadly weapons was victorious. In fact, the invention of increasingly lethal and devastating tools of war has largely driven the evolution of warfare, stimulating the development of new counter-weapons, strategies, and battlefield tactics. Among the major advances in ancient times were the composite bow, the war chariot, and the stone castle. Another was the Greek phalanx, a mass of close-packed spearmen marching forward as a unit, devastating all before it. In medieval times, the stirrup made it easier for a rider to stay on his horse, increasing the effectiveness of cavalry charges. And a progression of late medieval and modern weapons—including cannons, handguns, rifles, submarines, airplanes, missiles, and the atomic bomb—made warfare deadlier than ever.

Each such technical advance made war more devastating and therefore more feared. And to some degree, people are drawn to and fascinated by what they fear, which accounts for the high level of interest in studies of warfare and the weapons used to wage it. Military historian John Hackett writes:

An inevitable result of the convergence of two tendencies, fear of war and interest in the past, has seen a thirst for more information about the making of war in earlier times, not only in terms of tools, techniques, and methods used in warfare, but also of the people by whom wars are and have been fought and how men have set about the business of preparing for and fighting them.

These themes—the evolution of warfare and weapons and how it has affected various human societies—lie at the core of the books in Lucent's History of Weapons and Warfare series. Each book examines the warfare of a pivotal people or era in detail, exploring the beliefs about and motivations for war at the time, as well as specifics about weapons, strategies, battle formations, infantry, cavalry, sieges, naval tactics, and the lives and experiences of both military leaders and ordinary soldiers. Where possible, descriptions of actual campaigns and battles are provided to illustrate how these various factors came together and decided the fate of a city, a nation, or a people. Frequent quotations by contemporary participants or observers, as well as by noted modern military historians, add depth and authenticity. Each volume features an extensive annotated bibliography to guide those readers interested in further research to the most important and comprehensive works on warfare in the period in question. The series provides students and general readers with a useful means of understanding what is regrettably one of the driving forces of human history—violent human conflict.

Medieval Warfare: Romance vs. Reality

Of the various modes of warfare practiced in human history, that of Europe in medieval times is one of the more popular subjects among students, general readers, and scholars. Textbooks, novels, children's storybooks, movies, video and war games, and Internet sites are filled with the familiar images of mounted knights taking oaths to defend the weak and charging at one another with long lances; castles mightily resisting the onslaught of battering rams, scaling ladders, arrows, and cannons; courageous individual combats between warriors armed with huge broadswords and shields; and righteous struggles of Robin Hood-like heroes against evil lords exploiting defenseless peasants.

Horrendous Butchery

Unfortunately, despite the widespread popularity and familiarity of these depictions, they can often be misleading. First, they tend to play up the heroic and romantic aspects of medieval fighting, emphasizing such themes as the nobility of knighthood, royal pageantry, and the defense of honor and morality. This idealistic way of looking at war was passed from generation to generation in medieval and early modern times through verbal storytelling, music, and eventually written literature. In the words of scholars Clara and Richard Winston:

> The tendency to idolize the role of the young warrior took many forms. A whole literature developed— songs and romances centering on the figure of the knight. His bravery, purity, and fidelity [loyalty] were subtly shifted from the field of battle to the castle hall. His allegiance . . . to his lord was translated into the servitude of a lover to his lady. Figures from the past, like [the folk heroes] Roland, Charlemagne, and King Arthur, were drawn into this mythology. They, too, were described in these new exalted and emotional terms, which, of course, had no relation to their historical reality.[1]

Indeed, the reality of medieval warfare was more often quite unromantic and extremely brutal, bloody, and cruel. "Despite the theological admonitions [religious warnings] against it," military historians James F. Dunnigan and Albert A. Nofi point out, "the Middle Ages had an enormous propensity to accept cruelty and bar-

barity as a fact of life."[2] Most knights and other medieval warriors fought not for love or honor but to gain power, land, prestige, or money, either for themselves or their leaders. Justice, morality, and protecting the innocent were usually secondary considerations used conveniently to justify aggression and slaughter.

This painting by nineteenth-century English artist Edmund Blair Leighton illustrates the common and popular romantic image of medieval chivalry and honor.

Also, the battlefield was less an arena for displays of chivalry and more a place of horrendous butchery, as revealed by some graves recently excavated in Sweden. The remains of more than a thousand soldiers killed in a battle in 1361 reveal, as one observer described the scene,

the effects of crossbow bolts vertically piercing [armor], sword and ax cuts, and blows from maces and

This engraving of eleventh-century knights fighting shows the savagery of the medieval battlefield.

morning-stars (spiked balls attached by a chain to a handle). In one case the lower legs were severed, and several skulls exhibited deep cuts. The lower legs below the protection of shields suffered many deep wounds.[3]

Such horrors were not confined to formal combat. It was not unusual, following a battle, for men armed with knives and axes to move among heaps of fallen but still living knights and mercilessly slay them as they lay helpless in their heavy suits of armor.

The romantic myth of medieval warfare as colorful and chivalrous is also shattered by the routine rape, pillage, and killing of innocent civilians. A twelfth-century chronicle describes a typical scene of victorious troops raiding local villages:

Out in the front [of the army] are the scouts and incendiaries [fire-makers]. After them come the foragers . . . [and] soon all is in a tumult. . . . The incendiaries set the villages on fire and the foragers visit and sack them. The terrified inhabitants are either burned or led away with their hands tied to be held for ransom . . . money, cattle, mules, and sheep are all seized.[4]

Even worse, such outrages were perpetrated not only against enemy civilians but sometimes against fellow citizens. "While your troops might owe allegiance to [the local lord]," say Dunnigan and Nofi,

the only civilians they felt kinship with were those from their own village. So if they were willing to march through another one of [the lord's] villages many miles from their own, the troops still felt they were moving through "alien" territory and tended to act accordingly. . . . In medieval times, there were no police departments or media to report atrocities. A few dozen soldiers could come upon a village . . . and kill a few of the inhabitants, and no one would know about it except the surviving villagers.[5]

An Evolution of Military Affairs

Another misconception is that the weapons, strategies, and tactics of warfare were the same throughout medieval times, as well as across all of Europe during these centuries. First, the time period in question was very long. It began after the disintegration of the Roman Empire in the fifth and sixth centuries, which marked the end of ancient times; and it continued until the emergence of modern nations and modes of warfare in the sixteenth and early seventeenth centuries. In a sense, then, the roughly one thousand years comprising medieval times was sandwiched between ancient and modern times. And this is duly reflected in the roots of the term *medieval*; it derives from the Latin phrase *medium aevum,* meaning "the age in the middle." This, in turn, gave rise to the common synonym for medieval times—the Middle Ages.

During these many centuries, the techniques of warfare did not remain stagnant. Rather, weapons, armor, battlefield tactics, fortifications, and general approaches to war changed and varied over time as events and needs dictated. To defend against invading armies, some local lords erected castles and other fortifications. Their enemies countered by developing more effective siege methods, which in turn stimulated new and even more effective defenses. Meanwhile, new weapons, devices, and technology—among them the stirrup, the battle pike, and gunpowder— steadily transformed warfare, rendering older tools and methods obsolete. In short, military affairs evolved over time.

Lack of Organization and Uniformity

Similarly, warfare was not the same all across Europe at any given time, despite a largely shared origin—Rome. It is accurate to say that initially Europe inherited most of its military ideas, weapons, and tactics from the Roman realm, on the ruins of which the medieval kingdoms grew. Until their last century or so as a nation, the Romans had maintained large, well-trained armies run by efficient, professional generals and administrators. Such armies were well coordinated, moved great distances quickly, and implemented the policies of the central authority on the entire Mediterranean world.

By contrast, medieval Europe lacked such scope and organization. Early Europe was a large, culturally diverse sphere made up of a patchwork quilt of small, often backward kingdoms with different aims, problems, and policies. Accord-

Among the new weapons that evolved during the late Middle Ages were gunpowder and cannons, as portrayed in this 1484 illustration.

ingly, their methods of fighting developed to meet local needs and realities; there were few large-scale battles; and wars tended to be localized, short-lived, and hastily and haphazardly planned, utilizing whatever weapons and soldiers could be gathered together in a given spot at a given time. As noted military historian Archer Jones explains:

> Most Western armies formed themselves only for a particular campaign. A Western commander usually would not have in advance a clear idea of the forces he would have, even if many of them were mercenaries [hired soldiers] whose employment he had arranged. He would not know the total numbers, the proportions of light and heavy infantry and of cavalry, or the quality of his heavy infantry. When the commander had concentrated his army, he rarely had time to train it as a unit, but had to embark immediately upon the campaign, if only because supply difficulties compelled him to move promptly.[6]

For these reasons, each medieval realm or commander emphasized the weapons and style of fighting best suited to local needs or circumstances. For a long time the French built their armies around cavalry (mounted horsemen) who charged at and tried to run down enemy infantry (foot soldiers); the English relied on infantry armed with deadly longbows;

Viking raiders wielded huge axes they swung with two hands; and the Scots and Swiss developed formations of foot soldiers holding long pikes. Nearly all of these peoples used foot soldiers, horses, armor, bows, swords, and castles; however, except for castles, there was usually little uniformity from one time and place to another.

Truth More Interesting than Fiction

These facts show that many of the popular depictions of—and ideas about—medieval warfare are myths and misconceptions that bear little relation to the realities. On the positive side, that does not detract from the compelling nature of the subject. The old adage that truth is usually far stranger and more interesting than fiction certainly applies here. Medieval weapons, armor, battle tactics, castles, and sieges continue to attract and captivate millions of people across the world. As scholars Nicholas Hooper and Matthew Bennett write, this is partly because people recognize that warfare "is a worthwhile subject of study, since it has been one of the primary forces of human endeavor." Moreover, "all aspects of human society have been shaped for better or worse by warfare," and "all states owe their shape and a good deal of their political and economic structure to war." Finally, because most of today's European nations and their offspring grew out of the conflicts of the Middle Ages, "these observations are especially true of medieval warfare."[7]

CHAPTER ONE

Cavalry Weapons and Tactics

For a long time, most historians believed that mounted warriors dominated medieval warfare. However, it now appears that the vision of rows of heavily armored knights gloriously charging against either cavalry or infantry was a distorted—or at least exaggerated—view. Most contemporary military sources from the period were written by members of the ruling elite, who tended to be knights. Therefore, they concentrated on—and inflated—the importance of their own exploits while downplaying the role of lower-class foot soldiers, whom they looked on as inferiors. Such accounts understandably misled many modern scholars.

This does not mean that the role of cavalry in medieval warfare was unimportant. To the contrary, it was often just as important as infantry; and horsemen were used to one degree or another by all medieval European kingdoms. The most balanced and accurate way to view medieval cavalry is as one pivotal part of a larger combined arms system, that is, an approach to warfare in which cavalry, infantry, fortifications, and other factors worked together, each playing a crucial role.

The Rise of Frankish Cavalry

The use and impact of medieval cavalry can be conveniently divided into two distinct phases. The first phase occurred in the early part of the era, from the sixth through tenth centuries. Although horsemen could be found in most parts of Europe, their major development and employment occurred in France, the region that the Romans had called Gaul. Among the tribal peoples who overran the Roman Empire were the Franks, who settled in Gaul and gave their name to the region.

Two dynasties (ruling families) of Franks—the Merovingian and Carolingian—ruled France in the early Middle Ages; and both developed strong cavalry traditions. This was partly because many of the enemies the Franks faced had large units of horsemen. These included the

Avars, tribesmen from eastern Europe (originally central Asia), and the Muslims who had recently overrun Spain. The Avars had many fine mounted archers, and the Franks felt they had to have their own horsemen to counter them. Another factor that contributed to the Frankish emphasis on cavalry was the creation by the Romans of many large horse-breeding estates in Gaul. After Rome fell, the Franks inherited these estates and maintained them.

Over time, the Frankish horse-breeding estates naturally became the nucleus of an elite class of horse warriors. They were elite because they were well-to-do and either part of—or directly sponsored and supported by—the ruling kings and nobles. This was because horses were very expensive to breed and raise. Equipping and training a mounted warrior was also expensive. The result was that cavalrymen gained increasing social status and wealth, as well as land, which over time

This nineteenth-century English illustration captures the arrogance of the elite class of cavalrymen who played crucial military and social roles in medieval times.

THE INFLUENTIAL CAROLINGIANS

The Carolingian realm, centered in France, proved highly influential for the development and spread of medieval European culture, armor, weaponry, and fighting styles. In large degree, this was attributable to the military campaigns and conquests of the first three—and most successful—Carolingian leaders: Charles Martel, Pepin the Short, and Charlemagne. In 732, at Tours, in west-central France, Charles Martel defeated a large force of invading Muslims, a victory that may have spared Europe from Muslim domination. After making himself king of the Franks in 751, Pepin fought both the Muslims in Spain and groups of Christians who opposed the pope in Italy. Charlemagne, who ruled from 768 to 814, was the most ambitious and famous of the three. His realm eventually encompassed parts of what are now Belgium, Germany, and Italy, as well as all of France, and many people viewed it as a reborn Roman Empire. Indeed, in 800 Pope Leo III crowned Charlemagne "Holy Roman Emperor." But this empire soon fell apart, because Charlemagne's heirs fought among themselves and carved his realm into petty kingdoms.

contributed to their becoming a sort of landed aristocracy.

Early Armor, Weapons, and Tactics

The Frankish and other early medieval cavalrymen differed from the later variety—the full-fledged knights—in their armor, weapons, and tactics. Armor composed of heavy metal plates was a later development; by contrast, Frankish horsemen wore light armor made of mail, or rows of iron rings or scales either riveted or sewn together to form a heavy protective shirt. (The Franks and many other Europeans inherited mail from the Romans, who had used it for many centuries.) Mail provided a certain amount of flexibility at the expense of comprehensive protection. A mail shirt allowed the rider to maneuver his horse and use his weapons with ease, for example; but although the mail could deflect the glancing blow of a sword or arrow, it could not stop a forceful direct thrust or puncture.

For weapons, Frankish and other early medieval cavalrymen relied mainly on swords and spears—and sometimes bows, as in the case of the Avars. Generally, they swung and threw the spear overhand, although an underhand stroke might be used to jab at the back of an enemy foot soldier who was running away. These riders also sometimes carried shields. Needless to say, it took a great deal of flexibility and skill to hold and maneuver both the shield and horse's reins with one hand, while using a spear or sword with the other.

As for tactics, shock action—direct charges of large cavalry units against either cavalry or infantry—was extremely rare. This was partly because large battles were themselves rare occurrences. Also, early Frankish horsemen did not have the benefit of the stirrup, which helps a rider maintain his balance and position atop his horse. Without stirrups, shock action was difficult, as any significant impact could knock a horseman to the ground.

When stirrups were adopted in western Europe in the early eighth century, they made mounted warriors more formidable; but at the time shock action was still rare. Such horsemen were used mainly as scouts; to guard the flanks (sides) of traveling armies and chase off ambushers; to raid villages; to pursue fleeing enemies, both mounted and on foot; and occasionally to harass and attack the flanks and backs of enemy troops during a battle. Moreover, evidence suggests that at crucial moments in battle Frankish and most other medieval horsemen more frequently dismounted and fought on foot. According to University of Minnesota scholar Bernard S. Bachrach:

During the Middle Ages, most battles in the field saw most of the men who came to the battlefield on horseback dismount and fight on foot. Indeed . . . Carolingian horsemen were trained to do this through the late Roman training methods [that they had inherited from Roman military traditions]. . . . Even Norman [northwestern French] horsemen . . . who are considered to have been among the most accomplished mounted fighting men in western Europe, far more often than not dismounted in battle in order to fight on foot.[8]

The purpose of such dismounting, which transformed light cavalry into heavy infantry, was to strengthen the regular infantry against large-scale enemy attack.

Having dismounted, horsemen fight on foot against attacking infantry at the battle of Roncesvalles, fought between the Franks and Basques in 778.

The Age of Heavy Cavalry

The second major phase of medieval cavalry dates to the later, or High, Middle Ages, lasting from the eleventh through sixteenth centuries. This was the era in which most, but certainly not all, cavalry units were either manned or dominated by knights. These were heavily armored mounted warriors who formed a distinct social and landed aristocracy. As in the case of earlier, lighter cavalry, the use of heavy cavalry in battle was most pronounced in France, although knights existed all over Europe.

The knights played an important role in the feudal order (or system) that spread across Europe in early medieval times, taking a firm hold by the eleventh century. After the fall of Rome, society became increasingly localized in character. Petty kings, princes, dukes, barons, and other nobles exercised great power over their own small kingdoms or large estates. An important aspect of feudalism involved freemen who provided nobles with military service in exchange for land tenure. A soldier who worked for and was dependent on a king or other lord was called a retainer (or vassal).

Some of these soldiers, including many descendents of the original Frankish horse breeders, became knights. And some of these knights became lords with large estates and retainers of their own. A number of such retainers might live in and guard

A feudal lord dubs one of his men a knight. New knights were expected to serve the lord on any of his military campaigns.

their lord's castle in peacetime; others might earn manor houses and castles of their own, complete with servants and even minor retainers, usually foot soldiers. Moreover, in wartime it became customary for a knight to take along some of these followers to help and support him when on a military campaign. A unit made up of a knight and his retainers and other followers was called a lance. Many knights, as Hooper and Bennett explain,

> were waged [paid] members of a royal, noble, or episcopal [church-run] household. The knight needed a war horse, riding horse and pack animals, and servants. The principal aide was the esquire [or squire], often a mature servant rather than a boy apprentice, who had an auxiliary [supporting] combat role. From the late fourteenth century, a lance consisted of one heavy cavalryman with an armed servant, a page, and three to six variously armed infantry.[9]

A Rapid Multiplication of Armor

The main reason that such a cavalryman of the High Middle Ages is classified as "heavy" is that his armor was heavier and more protective than that of the lighter horseman of the Carolingian era. Beginning in the eleventh century, mail shirts became longer and heavier, for example. Typical was the hauberk, which stretched to the knees and featured a split up the lower-middle to allow the rider to mount his horse. Also common was the coif, a mail hood that covered the head; it often had a protective flap that could be drawn across the lower face. Soon, mail arm and leg coverings, as well as mail gloves, were added, increasing protection but also the overall weight of the outfit. Starting about 1150, most European knights also began wearing a loose cloth garment—the surcoat—over the mail suit.

This rapid multiplication of armor continued apace. By about 1200, many knights wore an iron cap under the coif to afford greater protection from lethal blows by broadswords and maces, or else a single-piece metal helmet; the most popular version was conical in shape but numerous other shapes existed. The trend toward solid metal protection continued as metal plates were riveted to the inside of hauberks and surcoats; and beginning in 1250, rounded metal plates appeared *over* the mail on knees, elbows, and other joints. The natural culmination of this trend was full plate armor, as well as armor for the horses, as Archer Jones describes:

> In the thirteenth century armored men began to use [metal] plates to strengthen their mail armor at particularly vulnerable points, such as the shin and knee. Gradually heavy cavalry added more and more plate . . . until a complete suit of plate armor, which protected the wearer from the shock of blows and deflected both hand weapons and crossbow bolts, became common. A helmet that completely covered the face had already been adopted. A suit of the new armor could weigh

These sketches show part of the evolution of protective armor. The man at left is clad totally in mail, while the knight at right wears mainly plate armor.

seventy pounds, and, together with its own armor, the horse had to carry over 100 pounds of metal alone. With a horse protected from lance wounds in the chest and the rider virtually proof against *harm*, the knight became far more formidable. However, this alteration both raised the cost of the mounted man and seriously reduced his mobility. The heavier burdened horse found it harder to gallop and the rider had difficulty in executing any maneu-ver but the straight-ahead charge. Dismounted, the rider could walk only with difficulty and had trouble climbing onto his horse and rising if he fell.[10]

Weapons and Tactics of Heavy Cavalry

The increasing weight and inflexibility of cavalry armor naturally made it more diffi-cult for riders to use the fairly wide array of weapons wielded by early medieval cavalry. The spear and bow were abandoned, therefore. The main weapon was now the sword—at first long, with a broad tip, and designed principally for slashing. In the twelfth century, as armor grew even heavier, sword tips grew thinner and more pointed, which increased their chance of penetrating mail.

The other main weapon used by European heavy cavalrymen was the lance. At first it was a simple, relatively light pole about ten to twelve feet long. But over time it grew thicker, heavier, and more tapered, broadening into a flared hand guard in the back. The key to the lance's effectiveness was the ability of the horseman to absorb a great deal of shock and stay mounted when the weapon hit an opponent. Although the stirrup provided some stability, it was not until the introduction of larger, wraparound saddles circa 1100 that cavalry charges with leveled lances

became a formidable offensive tactic. In what is referred to as the "couched lance technique," the back, or butt, of the lance rested on the saddle's pommel, which absorbed much of the shock of a strike. The late fourteenth century witnessed the introduction of a further improvement: Called the *arrĕt,* it was an extra support for the lance's butt built into the rider's metal breastplate.

With such effective armor and weapons, the shock action of heavy cavalry in the High Middle Ages could be truly formidable. The most effective use of such horsemen was in a combined arms assault against infantry. First, one's own archers and infantry softened up the opposing army, inflicting casualties and tiring the enemy; next the knights lowered their lances and charged the opposing infantry, dispersing them and opening up gaps; then one's own infantry rushed into the gaps

A group of eleventh-century knights engages in a session of friendly jousting. Although their stirrups provide some stability, the knights still lack the wraparound saddles needed for the couched lance technique.

and inflicted heavy damage, while the cavalry turned around and attacked the enemy's rear lines. (It should be pointed out that many late medieval European armies also used light cavalry units to back up their heavy cavalry; because the lightly armored riders were more flexible, they could perform certain tasks, such as chasing down fleeing enemy troops, better than the heavily armored ones.)

The Dangers of Overconfidence

Heavy cavalry was usually far less effective when used alone. This was because infantrymen who were tightly packed and well ordered, well armed, fresh and rested, and brave enough to stand their ground could inflict heavy casualties on armored horsemen. Also, because knights were part of the social elite, they were of-

ten arrogant and overconfident. This was especially true of French horsemen, whose cavalry traditions were the oldest and proudest in Europe. So it is perhaps not surprising that the French lost some major battles because they placed too much confidence in heavy cavalry, particularly when unsupported by infantry.

A classic example occurred in 1119. The French king, Louis VI, led a force of about four hundred knights into English-controlled Normandy (in northwestern France) and there encountered the English king, Henry I, with five hundred knights. Henry ordered four hundred of his horsemen to dismount and form an armored wall of heavy infantry behind the other hundred, who remained mounted. Then Louis unwisely ordered all of his men to lower their lances and charge the enemy. His knights managed to break

THE INTRODUCTION OF THE STIRRUP

The stirrup, one of the more important military innovations of medieval Europe, first appeared in China some time in the late first millennium B.C. It was originally intended to make mounting a horse easier, not to give the rider better balance and more secure seating, which ended up being its most important advantages. From China the device spread to India, where it came into use in the first century A.D. By the fourth century the stirrup had reached some parts of eastern Europe, where various tribal horsemen, eventually including the Huns and Avars, adopted it. It was not until the early eighth century that western

Europeans began using stirrups. The device made a mounted horseman more formidable because he could be surer of staying seated while wielding his sword, shield, spear, lance, or bow. Indeed, he might stay mounted even after receiving a heavy nonlethal blow from an opponent. He could also temporarily increase his height over an opponent by standing in his stirrups. However, the importance of the stirrup alone has been somewhat exaggerated. It took a combination of stirrups and special saddles and lances beginning in the eleventh century to make shock action and jousting on horseback practical.

A medieval illustration depicts a battle of the Hundred Years War. The English, at left, attack with a combination of infantrymen wielding longbows and both mounted and dismounted horsemen.

through the smaller force of English horsemen; but just as Henry had anticipated, this clash slowed the French charge almost to a halt. Protected by their heavy armor, the English knights who had dismounted swarmed around the French riders, pulling them from their horses and either killing or capturing them. A combination of heavy infantry and heavy cavalry had easily defeated heavy cavalry working alone.

Overconfident knights could also fare badly against new and lethal weapons. An important example was the English longbow, which came to the fore in the Hundred Years War, fought between France and England from 1337 to 1453. In August 1415, England's King Henry V launched an invasion of France, landing his army at the mouth of the Seine River. Large numbers of French knights marched north, vowing to crush the intruders; and in October the two armies clashed at Agincourt, south of Calais. According to historian and former prime minister of England Winston Churchill's account:

The French, whose numbers have been estimated at about twenty thousand, were drawn up in three lines of battle. . . . With justifiable confidence they awaited the attack of less than a third their number, who, far from home and many marches from the sea, must win or die. . . . The [English] archers were disposed in six wedge-shaped formations, each supported by a body of men-at-arms [horsemen]. . . . The whole English army, even the King himself, dismounted and sent their horses to the rear; and shortly after eleven o'clock on St. Crispin's Day, October 25, he gave the order [to advance]. . . . The archers . . . advanced to within three hundred yards of the heavy [French cavalry] masses in their front. They planted their stakes and loosed their arrows. . . . Under the arrow storm, [the French mounted knights] in their turn moved forward down the slope. . . . Still at thirty [rows] deep they felt sure of breaking the [English] line. But . . . the longbow destroyed all before it. [French] horse[men] . . . went down; a long heap of armored dead and wounded lay upon the ground, over which the reinforcements struggled bravely, but in vain. In this grand moment the [English] archers slung their bows [aside], and, sword in hand, fell upon the reeling

MANY KNIGHTS LACKED DISCIPLINE

Although heavily armored knights had many advantages in battle, they also had certain disadvantages. Their armor was very inflexible, for example, so if they fell to the ground they had trouble standing up unaided. As explained here by scholars James F. Dunnigan and Albert A. Nofi (in their Medieval Life and the Hundred Years War*), arrogance and lack of discipline were other disadvantages that could detract from a knight's overall effectiveness as a warrior.*

The knights believed their own propaganda. Foot soldiers were disdained [by heavy cavalrymen] and discipline was seen as incompatible with a noble warrior's honor. The basic problem was that every noble (knights and above in social rank) thought he was above obeying orders. A duke or a count had some control over his knights . . . but each such noble was less impressed by the royal official, or king himself, in charge of the entire army. Every noble thought he, and his troops, deserved the post of honor in the first rank. Any army commander would try and line up his various contingents in such a way that each would be used to best effect. Most knights (of whatever rank) simply wanted to get at an enemy and fight it out man to man. This was the mentality of knights through most of the medieval period.

squadrons and disordered masses [of fallen French knights].[11]

In the two to three hours the battle lasted, more than ten thousand Frenchmen died, while the English lost less than a tenth that number.

The End of Medieval Cavalry

Still, when properly used, heavy cavalry helped to win more battles than it lost; and it remained a crucial component of European armies for the rest of medieval times and even into early modern times. Changes continued, however. For example, certain factors eventually worked to reduce the amount and weight of the armor these riders wore. First, their armor continued to grow increasingly expensive, which severely limited the number of heavy cavalrymen a general could field. Second, these horsemen were useful only in massed charges in large battles, which were infrequent. The horsemen proved to be too specialized. "For scouting, foraging, guarding bridges and crossroads, and other mundane duties of ordinary campaigning," scholar Thomas F. Arnold points out, "lighter and less . . . burdened types of cavalry proved they could do the job both better and more cheaply."[12]

Also, by the late sixteenth century guns had come into wide use on the battlefield, and some bullets could penetrate all but the thickest and heaviest plate armor. For a while, the preferred countermove was to produce even heavier armor. But this proved impractical. The ultimate solution was to lighten or eliminate the armor, abandon the lance, and arm the riders themselves with guns, which essentially marked the transition from medieval to modern cavalry.

CHAPTER TWO

Infantry Weapons and Tactics

Infantry played an important role in warfare throughout the Middle Ages. Foot soldiers took many forms, including archers, swordsmen, spearmen, pikemen, and others. They also played roles of varying kinds and importance, depending on the situation, as well as following the military traditions of the local regions in which they lived.

In fact, some kingdoms and regions stressed the use of infantry much more than others. In England, for instance, no strong cavalry tradition evolved in early medieval times; so the English had few mounted horsemen and relied more on foot soldiers, especially archers, who became some of the most effective soldiers in all of Europe. Similarly, the Scots and Swiss had no cavalry traditions and became famous for their strong infantry units, which effectively utilized spears and pikes.

However, except for the Swiss armies, which were made up entirely of foot soldiers, even the best infantry units rarely won battles by themselves. In most of the few large pitched battles fought during the period, infantry was most effective and successful when used in combination with cavalry. Foot soldiers were more autonomous and important than cavalry during sieges, which were much more common than large showdowns on the battlefield. During a siege, infantrymen not only surrounded and attacked strongholds but also foraged for food and other supplies, ravaged surrounding villages, and burned enemy fortifications and other assets.

Whether deployed on the battlefield or engaged in sieges, infantry was generally divided into two broad groups: those who could afford weapons and did the bulk of the fighting; and the very poor, who did menial labor, including carrying equipment, setting up camps, digging trenches, and so forth. Very little is known about these laborers, because contemporary accounts were written by upper-class men who held the peasants in contempt and largely ignored them. So the following discussion is concerned primarily with the first group—the fighters, mainly in their battlefield capacity.

Raising Troops

Local kings and lords required the services of such fighters fairly often. So they needed a way to raise large numbers of foot soldiers reasonably quickly and with a minimum of difficulty. In the countryside, where people lived in landed estates or small villages, the solution was often a temporary militia, especially in the early medieval centuries. A militia is a part-time military force composed of farmers, workers, and other citizens. In an emer-

gency, they collect their weapons, assemble and fight, and then return to their private lives. About this general citizen levy, Bernard Bachrach writes:

The process of militarizing the civilian population in medieval Europe . . . was grounded on the assumption that all able-bodied men were responsible for defending their homes. . . . In addition, each man was to provide greater or lesser service on the basis of his wealth. Thus, all able-bodied men were required to serve in a general levy, a locally based militia for the defense of the region in which they

A late medieval woodcut shows armored foot soldiers fighting during the siege of a town. A contingent from the town has ventured outside the walls hoping to drive the enemy away.

MEDIEVAL CITY MILITIAS

In contrast to the foot soldiers in rural medieval militias, those in many European city militias tended to serve much longer. Evidence shows that the militias of the cities of northern Italy and Flanders (located north of France) were also better equipped and trained than rural levies. These qualities are attributable to the crucial and rigorous duties these men performed. They policed a city's streets, guarded its walls, defended those walls during a siege, and protected the trade routes leading into the city. Because the city's existence depended on these soldiers, they needed to be better trained and experienced than their rural counterparts; and adequate training and experience required longer terms of service.

lived. . . . The Anglo-Saxon [early English] version of the general levy, for example, often rather romantically labeled "the nation in arms," was the great *fyrd*.[13]

After the Norman conquest of England in the eleventh century, the English general levy was called the *Posse Comitatus*, or the "county force." Each local unit was under the command of an official called a sheriff. The French referred to their citizen militia as the *Arriére-ban*.

Under the feudal system in these realms, each manor, or country estate, had to support the levy by supplying a group of soldiers called a retinue. Typically, the number of foot soldiers in a retinue was much greater than the number of cavalry. In the 1300s, for example, an English noble named Richard Lord Talbot had a retinue that included fourteen knights, sixty squires, and eighty-two archers. All of these men likely lived and worked on the estate. Usually such soldiers served a term of forty days. They sometimes stayed on if a campaign lasted longer; but this was the exception rather than the rule, since most of those pressed into service were reluctant to leave their farms and families for too long.

Although the medieval levies played a crucial role in supplying infantry to prosecute wars, they had several drawbacks. First, the number of foot soldiers a king could raise via a levy was often smaller than what he needed. Also, the rural levies usually produced a large proportion of inadequately equipped and poorly trained men, most with little enthusiasm for serving.

Under these conditions, kings recognized that they had no choice but to supplement their homegrown militia with mercenaries, professional soldiers who hired themselves out to anyone willing to pay their price. Mercenaries were generally well armed, well trained, and battle hardened. And they usually served for as long as they were needed. So having a hard core of mercenaries in his army gave a king definite military advantages.

Eventually, beginning in Switzerland in the early fourteenth century, national standing (permanent) armies began to emerge. But these remained relatively few in number until the close of the Middle Ages. So levies and mercenaries continued to be used to some extent throughout the remainder of the period.

Armor, Weapons, and Tactics

Whether militia, mercenaries, or national forces, most medieval European foot sol-

diers usually wore much less armor than mounted troops did. For one thing, the average infantryman could not afford the elaborate armor worn by knights. Also, heavy armor would have weighed down a foot soldier, making him slower and less flexible.

Still, many infantrymen wore at least some armor. Typical was a light mail shirt and a metal helmet, often in the form of an

The foot soldier at left wears a metal helmet and leg protectors, as well as some mail armor beneath his jerkin. The one at right is too poor to afford armor and relies on several layers of linen for protection.

THE WIDESPREAD USE OF MERCENARIES

Mercenary foot soldiers hailed from nearly every corner of Europe and fought almost everywhere on that continent. However, certain regions were known for the availability and quality of their hired infantry. From the ninth to the eleventh centuries, Norway, Denmark, and other Scandinavian regions were major sources of these warriors. In the twelfth century, Flanders and its surrounding areas produced mercenaries who were known for their skill with the spear and short pike; and in the same period the Italian city of Genoa became famous for its hired crossbowmen. Later, Welsh, Irish, German, and Swiss mercenaries were widely employed. In the fourteenth century, some of these fighters formed small but disciplined and effective mercenary armies, each of which could be hired as a unit. The first well-known example was a force of some six-thousand Germans and Swiss led by Werner von Urslingen. Various Italian cities employed this group in the early fourteenth century.

iron cap with a wide brim. Those who could not afford mail wore quilted jerkins of linen or leather, sometimes with small metal plates sewn into them. Professional mercenary foot soldiers often could afford to wear metal breastplates and leg armor.

Medieval infantry carried a variety of weapons that varied from place to place and era to era. These included swords, daggers, spears, pikes, axes, maces, simple bows, crossbows, and eventually crude handguns, as well as shields of various sizes and shapes. There was rarely much uniformity, as soldiers wielded whatever they could afford or what was most readily available. The poorest foot soldiers sometimes used simple farm implements.

These poor farmers almost never played a significant role in pitched battles, however. They were not only inadequately equipped but also lacked armor and training. To provide such men, and indeed most other foot soldiers, with extensive training was in most cases out of the question. Most kings and lords lacked the financial resources to equip and train large standing armies in peacetime. And there was usually barely enough time during a campaign to drill even the best-armed infantry in basic tactics, especially offensive ones. It was fairly easy to teach a large group of men to stand in a mass and hold their ground against attack, but it was much more difficult and time consuming to drill them in the complex formations and maneuvers needed to go on the attack themselves. More often than not, therefore, regular foot soldiers played a rather static defensive role on the battlefield, largely trying to fend off assaults by mounted or dismounted cavalry. And the success of infantry in large battles, at least in the early Middle Ages, was often due as much to effective generalship and luck as to the types and qualities of weapons.

A clear example is the famous Battle of Hastings, fought in 1066 between the

English Saxons, led by King Harold, and the invading Normans, commanded by Duke William (later called William the Conqueror). Here, both sides were more or less evenly matched in infantry and either was capable of attaining victory. However, William used his foot soldiers, especially his archers, more effectively, while Harold's infantry made some serious tactical mistakes. Archer Jones gives this excellent account of the battle:

> Harold arrayed his force of heavy infantry in a strong defensive position along the hill with his flanks protected by the steepness of the ascent. . . . His men probably numbered between 5,000 and 11,000. . . . William marched to the enemy position in the morning and arrayed his army, which was probably about the same strength as Harold's. . . . William opened the battle by advancing his archers. . . . Pelted with a hail of arrows, the English line remained immovable. The heavy infantry attacked next but . . . failed to make an impression on the . . . thick English line. Then the heavy cavalry charged [but also made no headway and fell back]. . . . Perhaps without orders, the English infantry surged down the hill in pursuit and quickly the alert and resourceful

Duke William (with raised sword at center) leads his cavalry in a charge against English foot soldiers.

Duke William . . . led his middle division of cavalry against the flank of the English. . . . [The] Norman cavalry quickly and easily cut down the infantry that after leaving their position lacked any formation. Only a few escaped to their post on the hill. . . . William then sent his archers to shower the English with arrows and followed this with an attack of his entire force. He alternated missile and shock attacks, inflicting casualties and demoralizing a force that had to receive both forms of assault passively. . . . Finally, an arrow mortally wounded King Harold in the eye, and the remainder of the . . . exhausted English army gave way.[14]

The Sturdy Longbows and Yeomen

William's assault proved to be the last successful invasion of England, partly because the English infantry became much more effective in the three centuries following the Norman conquest. In fact, in weaponry, training, and organization, the English foot soldiers, called yeomen, were long second-to-none in Europe. This development can be credited to a few farsighted leaders, notably King Edward I and his immediate successors.

PILLAGE AND PLUNDER EXPECTED

When mercenaries finished a campaign, they often became brigands who pillaged and plundered the same realm they had just fought to protect. But mercenaries were not the only soldiers who ransacked manors and villages. Regular infantry often engaged in the practice as a regular and expected warfare tactic, as explained here by historians James F. Dunnigan and Albert A. Nofi (in Medieval Life and the Hundred Years War*):*

In most medieval armies, it was expected that the troops would "live off the land." This did not mean that they would go hunting and live off nuts and berries from the forest. . . . It meant that any food or other valuable encountered as the troops moved along was free for the taking. . . . Once on the lands of the enemy, pillage was encouraged. This not only demoralized the enemy population, but it made your troops happy and gave you the opportunity to skip a pay day and get away with it. Plunder was another matter. This was organized pillage, undertaken when there was a lot of wealth concentrated in one place and the nobles wanted to make sure they got their cut. Towns and castles were the most likely places to find plunder. . . . Not being allowed to plunder a town was a big disappointment to the troops. . . . Towns and castles often yielded tens of millions of ducats worth of coin and treasure. . . . In an age when the average working stiff was living well on an annual income of 3,000 ducats, this was good money indeed. And then there was all that opportunity to abuse the local women. Armies were never friendly . . . and the people in the towns and castles well knew it.

An eighteenth-century illustration depicts a medieval English bowman. This man was part of an elite unit, as most archers could not afford mail armor.

These leaders recognized that the lack of standardized infantry weapons and training was a serious problem. Their solution was to recruit large numbers of yeomen who owned a specific weapon—the longbow—and to pay them to train with that weapon during peacetime; that way, a force of highly trained infantry could be called on to fight in wartime. The English yeomen used various weapons besides the longbow, including swords, axes, daggers, and clubs. But these were mainly backup weapons they resorted to in the hand-to-hand fighting that occurred if and when the enemy managed to penetrate the English lines. Their main tool, the longbow, was often able to stop most attackers well before they reached those lines.

The reasons the longbow was so effective had little to do with its size; in fact, it was not much longer than an ordinary hunting bow. It also did not shoot arrows

CROSSBOWS AND LONGBOWS CONTRASTED

In this tract from his Castles: Their Construction and History, *Sidney Toy, an expert on medieval warfare, compares the effectiveness of crossbows and longbows in various combat situations.*

Among the hand weapons in use during the Middle Ages the bow and arrow still held a strong position, and that long after the introduction of the crossbow. . . . The crossbow was in general use [in Europe] by the end of the twelfth century and, except among the English, was the favorite [hand] weapon from that time to the latter part of the fifteenth century. In open warfare the English preferred the longbow, which was about 6 ft. long. The longbow was light while the crossbow was heavy and cumbersome. With the longbow the archer could shoot about five arrows while the crossbow was discharging one bolt, and he could keep his eye on the foe during the adjustment of a new missile, while the crossbowman's whole attention was required for this purpose. In the defense of fortifications, however, where the crossbowman would have support for his bow and himself be secure from attack, the crossbow, with its heavier missile, greater force, and longer range was by far the superior weapon. The effective range of the longbow was about 220 yards, that of the fifteenth-century crossbow was from 370 to 380 yards.

A medieval German crossbowman aims his weapon.

as far as a crossbow did. One factor that gave the longbow superiority over the crossbow in most pitched battles was its rapid fire. The longbow could fire several arrows in the same amount of time a crossbow fired one. "[Each] yeoman could let loose a dozen arrows a minute," write Dunnigan and Nofi, "creating a steady stream of deadly missiles. Advancing horsemen were doomed, as their . . . mounts went down from arrow wounds. The riders went down also, often with broken bones and other injuries."[15] Another factor was the longbowman's high degree of training. Dunnigan and Nofi continue:

> The king offered money, and other favors, to encourage peacetime training, and good pay when the yeomen were called into action. . . . The yeomen were skilled at more than just handling the bow. Their training concentrated on firing in groups . . . of 20 to 100 men. . . . The archers soon learned which angle to point their bows in order to land their arrows on a while sheet (the common target, representing a group of enemy troops) at different ranges.[16]

This combination of a deadly weapon and effective training proved itself repeatedly on the battlefield, especially during the Hundred Years War. Often, the French knights were unprepared for or discounted the abilities of English foot soldiers, whom they held in contempt. And the consequences of this arrogance were disastrous. Perhaps the classic example was in the first major battle of the war, at Crécy in 1346, in which the French first encountered massed English longbows. The English infantry won a stunning victory over the French knights and their supporting troops, mercenary crossbowmen from the Italian city of Genoa. This vivid account of the battle is from the *Chronicles* of the fourteenth-century French historian Jean Froissart.

> The Englishmen, who were in three battles [regiments] . . . saw the Frenchmen approach. . . . The lords and knights of France [were disorganized] . . . for some came before and some came after, in such evil order that one did trouble [get in the way of] another. . . . When the Genoese were assembled together and began to approach [the English lines] they uttered a great cry to abash [startle and frighten] the Englishmen, but these stood still and stirred not for all that. Then the Genoese a second time made a fell cry and stepped forward a little, but the Englishmen retreated not one foot. . . . Then they [the Genoese] shot fiercely with their crossbows. Then the English archers stepped forth one pace and let fly their arrows so . . . thick that it seemed [like] snow. When the Genoese felt the arrows piercing through their heads, arms and breasts, many of them cast down their crossbows. . . . When the French king saw them fly away he said, "Slay these rascals, for they shall . . . trouble us without reason." . . . Ever still the Englishmen shot where they saw the thickest press [of enemy soldiers]. The sharp arrows

The soldier at left wields a halberd (or poleax), while the man to his right carries a long spear.

ran into the knights and into their horses, and many fell, horses and men . . . and when they were down they could not rise again.[17]

The Deadly Swiss Pikemen

The other medieval European infantry that proved superior on the battlefield—the hedge (dense mass) of pikemen—also owed its success to the combination of a lethal weapon and intensive training and drilling. Spearmen were common foot soldiers across most of Europe in early medieval times. In the twelfth and thirteenth

centuries, some armies began to emphasize the spear over other infantry weapons, in the process making it longer and more specialized. The three main areas where this occurred were Scotland, Flanders (encompassing parts of what are now Belgium, the Netherlands, and northern France), and Switzerland. In Scotland and Flanders, ordinary six- or seven-foot spears grew into pikes twelve feet long; and the Swiss eventually wielded pikes eighteen feet long. Another similar weapon was the halberd (or poleax). A long spear with an axlike blade mounted near the end, it could be jabbed to penetrate mail armor or swung with two hands like a giant ax. One well-placed stroke of this weapon could bring down both a horse and its rider.

At first, such weapons were used mainly defensively, as many other medieval infantry weapons were. The men formed a tightly packed hedge with the pikes pointing outward, creating a formidable barrier that could blunt most cavalry charges. In this way the Scottish pikemen defeated the English cavalry at Bannockburn (in southern Scotland) in 1314. But such victories were possible mainly because the enemy made the mistake of relying on cavalry. Opponents were more successful when they employed massed

archers against the pikemen, who remained largely stationary and open to the deadly effects of missile barrages. "The spearmen of this date lacked speed and maneuverability," military historian Terence Wise points out. "Although they were strong on the defensive, they could not change front or formation easily and because of their limitations they could rarely win a battle on their own."[18]

For such infantry to realize their potential, the fighters needed to go on the offensive. The Swiss pioneered this approach beginning in the early fourteenth century. At first, they armed their all-infantry armies with halberds. But eventually they

A group of knights charge at but fail to make a dent in the mighty Swiss Gewalthaufen.

supplemented the halberds with long pikes. The Swiss basically revived the ancient Macedonian phalanx. This was a battle formation made up of soldiers standing in several rows, one behind the other, and carrying long pikes that projected from the front in a mass that resembled a porcupine's raised quills. The Swiss called their phalanx the *Gewalthaufen.* It was usually about twenty rows deep. According to scholar Douglas Miller in his book about medieval Swiss warfare:

> The first four ranks of pikemen would level their weapons to create an impenetrable wall, while the fifth and remaining ranks would hold their weapons upright, ready to fill in any gaps. Because of its length, the pike was held differently by each of the four ranks. The front rank would kneel down with the weapon held low, while the second stooped with the butt held under their right foot. The third rank held the pike at waist level and the fourth rank held it at head height. This classic defensive formation could stop any cavalry charge; and where the ranks of pikes were deeper and the weapons were held upright, such a forest of close-packed staffs could afford considerable protection against the fall of enemy arrows.[19]

The Swiss phalanx was even more devastating when it went on the offensive. The well-drilled men could move together swiftly and perform complex maneuvers, including changing direction almost at a moment's notice. Meanwhile, supporting the moving *Gewalthaufen* were units made up of men carrying halberds, crossbows, and by the early fifteenth century, crude handguns. These weapons usually softened up the enemy before the pikemen moved in for the kill. Not surprisingly, the Swiss armies were very successful, much feared, and remained Europe's premiere infantry until almost the end of the Middle Ages.

CHAPTER THREE

Siege Warfare: Castles and Fortifications

Castles and fortified towns dominated the political and social life of the Middle Ages, particularly in the period lasting from about 1000 to 1500. These were the places that the kings, lords, and other nobles lived. And from these strongholds they set social standards, collected taxes, oversaw food distribution, made laws, and dispensed justice to the thousands of ordinary people living in surrounding farms and villages. In the hands of an elite and powerful few, therefore, castles and other fortified places became instruments of political and social control.

Castles also dominated medieval military affairs. This was because the kings and lords who lived in them often did not get along with one another. Not surprisingly, complex and constantly shifting alliances and hostilities among competing nobles led to periodic attacks and counterattacks on and from fortified strongholds. "Enemy castles were major political-military objectives in themselves,"[20] write Joseph and Frances Gies, noted scholars

of medieval society. Another expert, Christopher Gravett, elaborates:

> Castles controlled the countryside around them; they provided bases from which . . . squadrons of knights could ride out to attack an enemy. If an invader chose to bypass such a stronghold, he left himself open to constant harassment, and to a threat hanging over his lines of communication and supply. Further, castles were often situated on roads or rivers and frequently near junctions; therefore if an invading body was of inadequate strength, it was forced to give such strongholds a wide berth, leading to major inconvenience and loss of time. In order to secure a conquered country, the castles themselves had to be captured.[21]

For these reasons, sieges of fortified places were by far the most common form of large-scale warfare in the Middle Ages.

A king's tax men collect coins from peasants outside a castle. Castles were potent tools for political and social control during medieval times.

The building of castles and fortified towns and the methods used to capture them were not new or unique to medieval times. Surviving relief sculptures and other evidence show that such fortresses and sieges were common in the ancient Near East, including the biblical lands, thousands of years ago. Later, the Greeks and Romans erected massive fortifications and developed siege warfare into a veritable art. It was from the Romans that the early medieval kingdoms inherited these concepts.

Like other kinds of conflict, medieval siege warfare had two main aspects: defense and offense. The defensive aspect, which must be considered first, was characterized by the strategic location and design of fortresses, as well as their construction. To ensure that sieges would fail, builders had to design and install features that would keep enemy soldiers from getting over, under, or through the walls. Moreover, new and innovative defensive measures had to be adopted from time to time in response to the ongoing development of more effective offensive siege devices.

Early Medieval Castles

The need for effective defensive measures existed from the beginning of the Middle Ages. Almost all Roman towns had been fortified to keep out enemies and marauders. And this practice carried over into early medieval society, as people continued to enclose their towns with massive walls.

On the other hand, medieval Europeans did not begin building individual castles in the countryside until the onset of the feudal age. The feudal order depended on a lord's ability to amass and maintain a strong power base from which to control his serfs and retainers. And an impregnable castle provided such a base.

The first primitive castles, constructed mainly of wood, appeared in northern France in the late ninth and early tenth

This engraving depicts some of the common defensive measures employed in castles, including high stone walls and a water-filled moat.

centuries. Thereafter feudal lords rapidly multiplied and grew more powerful. And by the tenth century, most of the lords of western Germany, Denmark, and especially Normandy were building the first "motte-and-bailey" castles. A motte was a conical hill varying from ten to one hundred feet in height and from one hundred to three hundred feet in diameter. The summit of the motte was protected by a wooden stockade, or palisade, probably made of boards or logs jammed vertically into the earth and braced by one or more rows of horizontal boards running around the perimeter.

Just below the motte, and also protected by a stockade, were one or more baileys (or wards), spacious open areas in which people, as well as horses, pigs, and sheep, could find shelter when an enemy threatened the surrounding territory. The twelfth-century French writer Jean de Colmieu described other features of these forts:

> It is the custom . . . [to] dig a ditch about [the motte] as wide and deep as possible. . . . Inside the enclosure is a citadel, or keep, which commands the whole circuit of the defenses. The entrance to the fortress is by means of a bridge, which, rising from the outer side of the moat and supported on posts as it ascends, reaches to the top of the mound.[22]

The general design of a motte-and-bailey allowed for defenders to fight first from behind the outer stockades that ringed the baileys. If and when such barriers were breached, they could retreat to the citadel atop the motte. The upper de-

fenses were more formidable, partly because their high vantage gave a clear view of enemy movements. More importantly, attackers faced the difficult task of advancing uphill, while arrows, rocks, and other missiles rained down on them.

However, a motte-and-bailey's best defenses were only effective in the short run, for the people confined in the cramped space inside the upper enclosure could not hold out for long periods of time. As scholar John Burke describes it in his study of medieval castles:

> Permanent residence at the top of the mound was neither easy nor desirable. There was little room to move about, sanitary conditions must have been deplorable, and it was a daunting task to carry food up from below and maintain adequate stocks in preparation for an emergency.[23]

Of course, during a siege it was impossible to acquire fresh supplies, so the prospect of starvation no doubt led to surrender on many an occasion.

Stone Walls and Shell Keeps

The next and much larger phase of castle building began in the eleventh century following the Norman conquest of England. After William the Conqueror crushed the Anglo-Saxons and killed King Harold in the Battle of Hastings in 1066, further opposition was minimal and William was able to assert nearly complete military domination of the country. Normandy had long been a main focus of castle building in Europe; and William brought the expertise needed for this art to England, which had

This sketch shows what England's Windsor Castle looked like in 1350. The original motte-and-bailey, erected about 1080, from which the rest grew, is visible in the center.

few heavily fortified strongholds before this time. In fact, it was the general lack of strong native English castles that contributed to the ease of the Norman conquest. Conversely, William's subsequent vigorous campaign of castle building ensured that his control of the land would be effective and permanent.

It is not surprising that the first Norman castles on English soil were timber motte-and-baileys like those in France. The first large version was built at Berkhamsted, twenty-five miles northwest of London, in the late autumn of 1066, to help secure London's surrender. But for the most part these structures proved to be stopgap measures. Their builders recognized early

on that the wooden gates and stockades were susceptible to fire damage. So the Normans began replacing the wooden enclosures with stone walls.

The new type of structure was called a "shell keep," basically a single circular wall enclosing an inner bailey atop a hill. It typically had small living quarters, workshops, stables, and storerooms that lined the inside of the wall, with its doors opening into the bailey. In more advanced versions stone towers, or inner keeps, which were usually substantially taller than the outer walls, were erected in the centers of the baileys. And several other defensive features were added to increase security and sustain the residents during a siege.

The shell keep at Restormel, in English Cornwall, of which large sections have survived, is an excellent example. The main shell wall is surrounded by a wide, deep moat designed to discourage attackers from reaching the walls. Within the shell itself is another ring wall, concentric to the first, surrounding a circular inner court; the distance between the two ring walls is just over eighteen feet. In that space, cross-walls create separate rooms and apartments, most two stories high. Originally located on the ground floor were cellars for storing large quantities of food and arms, while the upper floor contained the living quarters.

The High Cost of Security

The importance of such major security features to the landed nobles cannot be over-stated. Without large-scale, effective defensive measures, the probability of a castle falling into enemy hands during wartime was high. And that might well mean the death of the castle's lord and his relatives and close supporters. Even worse, it might result in the eradication of their family lines and/or the absorption of their estates or the whole kingdom by a rival realm.

The degree to which the nobles took this threat seriously is revealed by the enormous sums of money they invested in castle construction. According to Dunnigan and Nofi's research:

> Even a simple stone tower could be incredibly expensive. A plain tower erected at Dover [in southern England] between 1180 and 1190 cost some 2.4 million ducats, at a time

A NORMAN SHELL KEEP

In this excerpt from his noted book on castles, scholar Sidney Toy describes the Norman shell keep at Launceston, in the southwestern English district of Cornwall. It was originally built as a motte-and-bailey in about 1080; the shell wall was added about a century later; and the inner tower about 1240.

The keep at Launceston is composed of an ovoid-shaped shell and a round tower . . . inside the shell. Here the shell . . . is 12 ft. thick and 30 ft. high, and has a deep battered plinth [course of foundation stones] crowned by a round molding. The wall walk was reached by two mural stairways, one near the gateway and one on the opposite side of the keep. . . . The keep is approached up the steep mound, which investigation has proved to be a natural hillock [as compared to those mottes that were artificially constructed], by a long flight of steps, formerly flanked by walls and covered in by a roof. The foot of the stairway was guarded by a round tower, and at the head stood the . . . entrance to the keep which was later protected by a portcullis [a wooden grille strengthened by iron]. . . . Considering its commanding position, its three lines of defense, and its magnificent middle platform [inner tower], this keep when complete must have been amongst the most formidable in England.

when crown [i.e., the king's] income in England was probably no more than 12 million ducats a year. As stone was fairly cheap (one or two ducats per hundredweight), the principal element in the cost was labor, which is why construction was stretched over ten years. If one wanted a more elaborate castle, and one wanted it in a hurry, costs would escalate rapidly. Thus, Chateau-Gaillard, the great bastion erected by England's Richard the Lionhearted on the Seine [River in France] . . . was put up in a single year, 1197–1198, at a cost of 12,721,800 ducats, of which some 75 percent went for labor, representing some 2,544,436 man-days, the equivalent of over 6,000 men for a year. Materials, on the other hand, ran only about 2.4 million ducats, and transportation for such was only about a million ducats more. When Edward I of England bound Wales between 1277 and 1302 with a chain of ten of the greatest castles ever built, his total investment ran to something approaching 90 million ducats. Of course, money expended on castles was well spent, for they were great long-term investments in military security.[24]

Such costs did not cover maintaining and guarding a castle once it was built, of course. A lord also had to keep a garrison (manned military installation) of well-trained soldiers on duty to defend the place in case of a sudden attack; in such an event, these troops would take necessary defensive actions while the lord rallied his supporters and allies. In England and many other areas, many of the soldiers who formed a castle garrison were retainers and other local men dependent on the local lord. They performed this duty as part of their feudal obligation to provide him with military service in exchange for land or other favors. The terms of service in a garrison varied from place to place, but the average was three months per year. Many soldiers disliked castle duty, viewing it as less prestigious than fighting in the field. So they paid the lord a scutage, a fee or tax with which he hired mercenaries to guard the castle.

Ideas from the East

Such feudal obligations, along with the castles that reinforced and perpetuated the feudal order, made the landed nobles in England, France, and elsewhere quite powerful in the years immediately following the Norman conquest. Yet their power, which rested in large degree on the quality of castle defenses, had far from reached its limit. The design and technology of their defenses continued to improve, which in turn stimulated the development of new siege devices, both of which made siege warfare more prevalent and more devastating.

These continued improvements in castle defenses were mainly the result of new construction ideas and techniques filtering across Europe from the Near East, the birthplace of stone fortresses. Especially influential in this regard were growing Western contacts with the Byzantine Empire and Palestine, both distinguished by their long tradition of

The remains of Chateau Gaillard, completed by English king Richard I in 1198. Chateau Gaillard remained one of Europe's greatest castles for centuries afterward.

building elaborate stone fortifications. In 1096, a number of European kings and lords responded to the pleas of Pope Urban II to go to Palestine and liberate Christian holy sites from Muslim control. This ignited the first of the several so-called Crusades that spanned the late eleventh through fourteenth centuries. One crucial result of these ventures was

that Christian knights were impressed by and immediately began to copy the eastern fortifications they encountered. According to Frances and Joseph Gies:

Of the peasants and knights who tramped or sailed to the Holy Land and survived the fighting, most soon returned home. The defense

SKILLED MASONS ERECT A SHELL KEEP

Construction techniques for shell keeps were fairly straightforward and uncomplicated. Although the noble owners of these early castles dictated their location and overall layout, it was the local stonemasons and carpenters who did the actual work; and these craftsmen used methods based partly on traditions that had been passed from one generation of builders to another from earlier cultures. Most commonly, flat rectangular stones or bricks were piled on top of one another in the age-old manner. However, some slightly more sophisticated masonry styles were used for parts of many shell keeps. The most prominent example was herringbone masonry. In such stone work, the material making up each course of stones was applied at an angle of about forty-five degrees. The mason tilted the stones in each succeeding course in the opposite direction of the one beneath it to make the stone grip and hold one another in place. Two courses of such stones bear a strong resemblance to herring bones, hence the name of the technique. This method of construction was employed by the Romans all across Europe and the English Saxons before the Norman conquest, as well as the Normans themselves.

A medieval woodcut shows masons laboring to erect a shell keep.

of the conquered territory was therefore left to a handful of knights—primarily the new military brotherhoods, the Templars and the Hospitallers. Inevitably their solution was the same as that of William the Conqueror, but the castles they built were from the start large, of complex design, and of stone. The crusaders made use of the building skills of their some-

time Greek allies and their Turkish enemies, improved by their own experience. The results were an astonishing leap forward to massive, intricately designed fortresses of solid masonry.[25]

Among the crusaders' principal eastern influences were the enormous and sophisticated walls and towers protecting the Byzantine cities of Constantinople, Nicaea, and Antioch. As they marched through Asia Minor, what is now Turkey, on their way to Palestine, the Europeans also saw seemingly impregnable Byzantine stone castles built at strategic points in the countryside. These forts quartered garrisons of cavalry and foot soldiers on a full-time basis, forces that could

Medieval illustrations show the formidable walls of Nicaea (left) and Constantinople (below). These mighty bastions made a strong impression on European crusaders.

FEUDAL VOWS ENCOURAGE THE SPREAD OF CASTLES

A brief examination of how the feudal order worked reveals that it influenced the steady and widespread proliferation of castles. A castle's lord and his loyal followers, called retainers (or vassals), cemented their bond in a solemn public ceremony of "homage," a term derived from the French word for man—*homme*—signifying that the retainer was to become the lord's "man." The retainer placed his hands in the lord's hands and swore fealty, or loyalty. This created a pact in which the retainer performed certain obligations, particularly to defend and fight for the lord. In return, the lord promised land use, protection, or financial assistance, or all of these. If a lord was especially rich and powerful, he possessed more than enough land to give away to his retainers. Many of these men, in turn, had more land than they could effectively exploit. One solution was for a retainer to distribute part of his land among others, who became his own retainers. As time went on, therefore, many of a lord's retainers ended up with their own substantial lands. Having become lords in their own right, some built castles on their newly acquired lands, strongholds that, ironically, eventually allowed them to compete for power with their former lords.

swiftly move out and intercept an enemy force attempting to penetrate imperial territory.

Murderesses, Moats, and Preemptive Strikes

In addition to learning strategic lessons about castles, the crusaders also borrowed design and construction ideas. An example of a specific feature they copied from Byzantine models was machicolation, the outward projection of a wall at the top of the battlements. Missiles or boiling oil could be dropped onto attackers through openings in the floors of such projections. Stone machicolation, which was not susceptible to fire damage, soon became common in castles throughout Europe. Among other castle features that spread from East to West was the portcullis, the heavy vertical gateway door used extensively by the ancient Greeks and Romans. Such doors were usually made of thick wood reinforced with iron plates and moved up and down via chains attached to a winch that was operated from a small chamber above the main gates.

Arrow loops were another popular feature introduced from the East. Bearing the nickname murderesses, these narrow vertical wall slits allowed castle archers a high degree of protection while they shot repeated volleys of arrows at approaching enemy troops. In principal, arrow loops were similar to crenellation, the succession of notches (merlons) and spaces (crenels) at the tops of battlements, a feature already long employed in European castles. Defending archers alternated at hiding behind the notches and firing through the spaces. But arrow

A typical medieval European drawbridge as seen from both the outside and inside. Winches retracted the chains, pulling the wooden bridge into an upright position.

loops had a design advantage that made them even more effective than crenellation, namely that on the outside the loops presented a very narrow, difficult target to attackers, while on the inside they flared outward, giving the defenders plenty of room to move around and command a wide field of fire. Throughout the twelfth and thirteenth centuries, European builders employed arrow loops on new castles and added them to existing ones.

Still other features that improved and strengthened European castle defenses included improved versions of two very old ideas: drawbridges and barbicans, both designed to defend a castle's main gate. A drawbridge was a wooden platform that spanned the moat and could be drawn back in an emergency, forcing attackers to enter the moat to reach the gate. Early versions simply slid back from the moat and remained in a horizontal position on the ground in front of the gate. Later, chains were attached to the outer ends of the bridge and, by means of winches, retracted into a chamber over the gate. When the chains were fully retracted, the bridge stood vertically against the face of the gate, creating an additional barrier to penetration. Other versions used various arrangements of pivots and counterweights to raise and lower the bridge.

A medieval barbican, like versions seen at Troy (on Asia Minor's western coast) and numerous other ancient Near Eastern sites, was an outwork or forward extension of the gate's walls. The barbican's walls often formed a separate enclosure outside the castle's main walls; and sometimes a barbican had its own fortified gate. The tactical advantage of such an enclosure was that attackers first had to enter it before they could reach the main gate. And once inside the barbican they were subjected to a deadly rain of missiles from the battlements at the tops of its walls. Some of the more elaborate castles had multiple barbicans. A notable example is Conway Castle, built by Edward I in northern Wales. Both the eastern and western gates are screened by lofty barbicans, one with its own strong gate and drawbridge.

A Fortified Base

Such innovative and imposing defenses were indeed impressive and afforded a very high degree of security. Yet it would be a

FORMIDABLE TOWN DEFENSES

Like castles, many medieval towns were protected by formidable fortifications that made besieging them a long and bloody endeavor. In this excerpt from Daily Life in the Middle Ages, *noted scholars Clara and Richard Winston describe such town defenses in medieval France.*

The new walls built around French towns were well-nigh impregnable. They were very thick, with an inside and outside course of stone and rubble between. Topping the walls were battlements—tall stone curbs behind which bowmen could crouch to shoot their arrows through narrow apertures [openings]. At intervals the walls were supplemented by towers. Bounding up the staircases inside these towers, the defenders could quickly and safely reach the top of the walls and be ready to grapple with an attacking party. Stones were hurled and boiling water poured down as the attackers struggled up their ladders. The entrances into the towns were shielded by gates and heavy metal grills called portcullises. There was also a drawbridge raised and lowered by pulleys. Walls were further protected by a wide, deep moat. This could be filled with water brought from a nearby stream via a canal or be left dry and allowed to grow up to rough briers. Perpetual watch was kept from the high towers flanking the principal gate, and the town was locked up every night even in peaceful times.

mistake to assume that a castle's defenders planned to just sit behind the walls and wait for the enemy to attack. Indeed, Gravett points out, a castle was "a fortified base from which armed men could ride out."[26] In many cases, the defenders prepared in advance to launch preemptive strikes on the enemy in hopes that a siege could be avoided. In 1119, for example, the garrison of Tillières Castle, near Paris, ambushed a group of troops on their way to attack the castle and thereby prevented a siege.

However, the majority of armies intent on capturing a castle did make it to the target and initiate a siege. When this occurred, both sides could expect to sustain casualties. Castle defenses were often formidable. But the offensive weapons of siege warfare were at times equally formidable and often frighteningly lethal.

CHAPTER FOUR

Siege Warfare: Offensive Weapons and Methods

Castles were usually the regional strongholds, supply depots, and power centers of medieval kings, lords, and other military strongmen. As Joseph and Frances Gies point out: "Always ready, requiring little maintenance and repair, demanding scant advance notice of impending attack, the castle remained the basic center of power throughout the Middle Ages."[27]

It is not surprising, therefore, that these formidable fortresses became the prime targets of attack in wartime, and thousands of sieges were mounted during the medieval era. Such operations failed as often as they succeeded, however, because capturing a castle was no easy task. More often than not it required hundreds, sometimes even thousands, of soldiers, carpenters, metalsmiths, laborers, missile weapons, and siege devices (catapults, battering rams, and so forth), as well as huge amounts of food and other supplies. All of these people, weapons, and sup-

plies had to be gathered, transported to the site of the siege, coordinated, and kept focused on the main task for weeks and sometimes months. To carry out these key organizational tasks, the lord conducting the siege needed numerous experienced senior and junior officers. Often these were professional mercenaries who had taken part in many sieges. Many of the soldiers might also be mercenaries.

These men had to be paid, of course. Also, the food and other logistical supplies did not come cheap. So sieges were enormously expensive ventures, especially if they lasted more than a few weeks. And it was not unusual for the besieger eventually to run out of money, forcing him to abandon the operation. "Say an army of 1,000 men approached [a castle]" Dunnigan and Nofi write, who were

mercenaries, costing the attacker, on average, 170,000 ducats a week to maintain. It would take several weeks to invest [surround] the place, build siege machines . . . and start digging tunnels [under the walls]. By this time the cost would already be up to half a million ducats, with less than a hundred thousand gained from pillaging the surrounding coun-tryside. . . . The besieger had to decide when to stop throwing good money after bad. We may not think of medieval warlords as accountants, but they had to pay their bills, too. Unpaid troops tended to drift away, leaving you defenseless in hostile territory. It wasn't all adventure and

The army of England's King Henry III lays siege to the castle of a rebellious lord in 1224. Attacking and taking castles became both an art and a major goal of warfare.

The battlements of Chepstow Castle, in south Wales, are extremely well preserved. The structure was particularly strong because it was built atop a base of solid rock.

glory. A lot of medieval warfare was the headaches delivered via a clerk's report on your current cash position.[28]

Sapping Operations

Whether an attacker eventually gave up and went home or continued a siege to its conclusion, the offensive methods used were more or less standard throughout Europe during most of the Middle Ages. As a siege began, the attackers naturally directed their best efforts toward exploiting the castle's structural weaknesses. Although there were usually few such vulnerable points, a stubborn and vigorous enough assault on them had at least a chance of success.

The most common built-in weakness of many castles was that they were erected over soft subsoil. The ideal was for a fortress to rest on a large outcropping of solid rock. And a few did, including mighty Chepstow Castle, near the border of England and Wales. If not, at least some of a castle's walls were vulnerable to sapping, or undermining. The usual procedure was to dig a long tunnel, aiming if possible at a tower or corner in a defensive wall. John Burke explains:

STEPS IN MOUNTING A SIEGE

In his informative book about medieval castles, scholar Philip Warner provides this list of the traditional steps, some or all of which attackers followed when preparing and executing the siege of a castle or other fortified place:

1. Forment dissension in the surrounding district so that crops would be destroyed and potential opponents killed by each other.
2. Attract as many local supporters and traitors as possible, luring them by the promise of plunder.
3. Build a second motte [i.e., temporary fortified place] a short distance from the castle under attack.
4. Set up siege engines within range of targets.
5. Set the miners digging trenches under the walls.
6. Fill in all ditches and moats, and bring siege towers up to the walls.
7. Create diversions while ladder parties try to scale walls.
8. Bring up battering rams and begin work on walls and gateways.
9. Aim stones from siege engines at points in walls that appear vulnerable.
10. Arrange for archers and slingers to sweep the battlements with continuous fire.

Driving a passage through dangerously unstable earth, the sappers used timbers to prop up the roof. . . . When they reached the target area, the tunnel was packed with branches, brushwood, rags, grease—anything which would burn—and the whole mass set ablaze.[29]

Beginning in the early fifteenth century, barrels of gunpowder were often substituted for branches and other traditional combustibles. Miners learned to build a few zigzags in a tunnel to protect them from the blast as they crawled away. "The sappers retired as speedily as miners always do when a charge has been fired," Burke continues:

If all went well, the timbers . . . collapsed, and into the weakened earth

collapsed also a wall tower or a corner of the keep itself. Once such a breach had been made, the assault forces were concentrated there.[30]

The operation just described sounds fairly easy and straightforward. In reality, however, sapping was a slow, painstaking process. When England's King John besieged Rochester Castle in 1215, for example, the mine his men dug, although ultimately successful, took over six weeks to complete. Sapping was also uncertain and dangerous. Sometimes the diggers' aim was off and they ended up in the wrong place; while even more often their tunnels prematurely collapsed, burying them alive. The remains of an abandoned sap, from a siege that took place in the summer of 1174, can still be seen at Bungay Castle in Suffolk (in eastern England).

Scaling Ladders and Siege Towers

Sapping was only one of several offensive methods of assaulting a castle. If the fortress was poorly manned, or if the attackers greatly outnumbered the defenders, scaling ladders might be used to gain entry. "The whole art of using a scaling ladder was speed," scholar Philip Warner writes:

> A good climber was up a ladder before the defender could dislodge its hooks from the battlements, and there were usually half a dozen crossbowmen or slingers [fighters

This nineteenth-century engraving showing medieval siege towers is highly exaggerated. In reality, the towers and troop sizes were usually smaller.

who used slings to hurl rocks or lumps of metal, often with considerable accuracy] to give covering fire.[31]

However, a great many ladders and men were needed for such an attack; and the assault had to be very well coordinated and intense. Moreover, even when besiegers met these conditions, they had to expect heavy casualties. The defenders used arrows, rocks, and boiling liquids to knock the attackers off the ladders and forked sticks to push the ladders away from the walls. Also, some climbers simply lost their balance and fell off. At an English siege of a French castle in 1346, an English officer fell from a scaling ladder and landed, badly hurt, in the dry moat. The French on the battlements quickly threw bundles of burning straw over him, roasting him alive.

To avoid, or at least reduce, the number of such casualties, attackers often built wooden assault towers, called "belfries," "bears," or other colorful names. These were often identical in many ways to some of the siege towers employed by the Greeks and Romans in ancient times. The towers were almost always assembled from materials gathered from the general vicinity. They gave the besiegers the advantages of height (since they stood at least as high as the castle's walls) and adequate cover from enemy fire (because the wooden sides proved effective shields). Also, a large tower could deliver an enormous amount of offensive fire. One such belfry, used in 1266 at the siege of Kenilworth Castle, in westcentral England, held two hundred troops and eleven catapults.

Yet siege towers, too, had their disadvantages. First, they were extremely heavy and difficult to move over rough ground or uphill. And because they were composed mainly of wood, the defenders could—and often did—set them ablaze. What is more, towers could not be wheeled over a moat. To eliminate this barrier, besiegers sometimes filled in the moat with debris. While doing so they were open to a shower of missiles from the walls, so they approached slowly in heavily protected wheeled shelters known as "cats," "rats," "tortoises," or "hedgehogs." Yet these shelters were not invulnerable either. Huge stones dropped from above sometimes penetrated them; and their wheels could break, leaving the men inside trapped near the castle walls. Despite the formidable firepower that siege towers delivered, therefore, even the largest and best equipped did not guarantee success. For example, the attack of the great belfry at the Kenilworth siege failed, and the castle surrendered only after disease ravaged the defenders.

Artillery Engines

When a castle was particularly strong, besiegers often either abandoned the above methods or supplemented them with artillery—siege machines that hurled stones and other projectiles at or over the walls. Several types of sophisticated artillery engines developed in Europe in the eleventh and twelfth centuries (influenced by eastern models, which themselves had been inherited from Greek and Roman times). All were constructed of wood, which meant that the

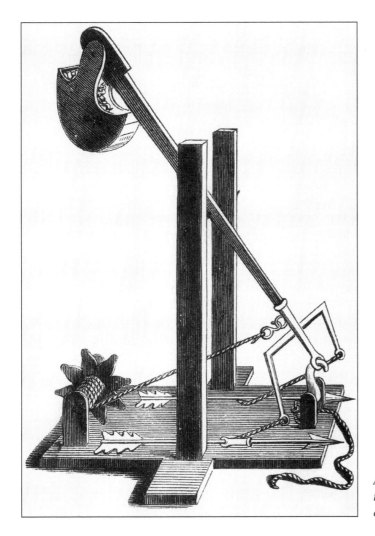

A woodcut depicts one of the many styles of medieval catapult.

attacking army had to bring along or find many skilled carpenters. During one of his military campaigns, England's King Henry II assembled over five hundred carpenters to build the artillery he needed to attack a rebel castle.

Among the most common artillery engines were the ballista, essentially a giant crossbow or spear-thrower, and the mangon, or catapult, which hurled large rocks. They operated on the principles of greatly increasing either the torsion (twisting) of ropes or the tension (stretching) of wooden levers; the burst of energy produced by suddenly releasing the ropes or levers sent the projectile on its deadly flight. A large mangon could hurl heavy rocks up to thirteen hundred feet. Even more devastating was the trebuchet, introduced into western Europe in the twelfth century and here described by scholar Hugh Braun:

A CASTLE'S WALLS
BORED AND BATTERED

Two of the more common devices used to breach walls in medieval times were bores and battering rams. A bore was a long, heavy wooden beam with a pointed iron tip at the end. A group of men placed it against a castle wall and, using handles, turned it like a screwdriver until it drilled a hole in the masonry. A battering ram was usually a large tree trunk that many soldiers (up to sixty or more in some cases) repeatedly smashed against a castle's doors or walls. When possible, the battering ram was fitted with an iron head and hung from a wooden framework so that the men did not have to hold it up while guiding it forward. Of course, it was usually necessary to protect the operators of bores and battering rams from missiles rained down by the defenders. The most common method was to place the devices and their operators inside wheeled wooden structures called penthouses.

This was a huge affair of great timber balks [beams] built up into a lofty trestle, at the summit of which was supported a long balanced beam. The shorter end of the beam was weighted with a large box of earth or stones. The longer end, which held the projectile, was hauled down in the same fashion as . . . the mangon; when released, the weight revolved the beam and flung the projectile. Its velocity was generally increased by the attachment of a long leather sling to the end of the beam. These trebuchets could throw a projectile weighing perhaps half a ton, and ranges of a quarter of a mile are recorded. The deadly feature of the trebuchet, however, was its high trajectory, which enabled it to hurl its projectiles over the top of any stockade.[32]

The frightening and lethal rain of missiles from these large artillery pieces is described in some surviving medieval tracts.

"At last the large machine was put up," wrote the thirteenth-century German chronicler Henry of Livonia, "and great rocks were cast at the fort. The men in the fort, seeing the size of the rocks, were seized with great terror."[33] At another siege, at Fellin, in Estonia, Henry said:

> The Germans built a machine, and, by hurling stones night and day, they broke down the fortifications and killed innumerable men and animals in the fort, since the Estonians had never seen such things and had not strengthened their houses against such attacks.[34]

Such siege devices, especially the trebuchet, were also used to fling diseased animals into castles in hopes of infecting the defenders.

Combining many different assault techniques and machines and pressing the attack relentlessly and vigorously often achieved the desired goal within a few weeks or months. The following vivid account of a successful siege is taken from a medieval chronicle known as the *Annals of Dunstable*. In 1224, after eight weeks of almost constant offensive operations, the castle of Lord Falkes de Bréauté's castle at Bedford (about forty miles north of London) fell to the forces of King Henry III.

> On the eastern side was a stone-throwing machine and two mangons which attacked the [new] tower every day. On the western side were two mangons which re-duced the old tower. A mangon on the south and one on the north made two breaches in the walls nearest them. Besides these, there were two wooden machines erected . . . over-looking the top of the tower and the castle for the use of the crossbow-men and scouts. In addition there were very many engines there in which lay hidden both crossbow-men and slingers. Further, there was an engine called a cat, pro-tected by which underground dig-gers . . . undermined the tower and

Soldiers use scaling ladders to reach windows in a defensive wall. Such ladders were effective when used in large numbers, but the attackers usually suffered heavy casualties.

castle. Now the castle was taken by four assaults. In the first the barbican was taken, where four or five of the outer guard were killed. In the second the outer bailey was taken, where more were killed, and in this place our people captured horses . . . crossbows, oxen, bacon, live pigs and other things beyond number. But the buildings with grain and hay in them they burned. In the third assault, thanks to the action of the miners, the wall fell near the old tower, where our men got through the rubble and amid great danger occupied the inner bailey. Thus employed, many of our men perished. . . . At the fourth assault . . . a fire was set under the tower by the miners so that smoke broke through into the room of the tower where the enemy were; and the tower split so that cracks appeared. Then the enemy, despairing of their safety . . . yielded [surrendered] to the king's command.[35]

The Defenders' Predicament

The ability to withstand a fully mounted siege like the one that overwhelmed Bedford Castle depended on several factors. Among these were the strength of the castle's walls, the size of its garrison, the amount of supplies it had stored, and the courage and determination of the defenders. Even if the inhabitants managed to beat back many assaults, the possibility of ultimate defeat was still high. Once surrounded, a castle with many people and animals cramped inside and possessing

few supplies soon faced the prospects of starvation, malnutrition, and disease. Desperate defenders were known to resort to eating their horses and dogs, and eventually mice, rats, and grass. The attackers often managed to poison the castle's well. Or the well dried up from overuse; this was the cause of the fall of Exeter Castle (170 miles southwest of London) in 1137 after a three-month-long siege. Moreover, under such crowded conditions the latrines usually backed up, increasing the likelihood of sickness and producing a foul stench. Morale was another important factor. During a siege, Fiona MacDonald and Mark Bergin write:

> The castle defenders lived in a state of constant uncertainty. They were cut off from contact with the outside world, and so did not know how well, or how badly, their allies were faring. The enemy forces camped outside the walls would do their best to depress them, by jeering, or by spreading false rumors.[36]

Suffering and deprivations like these, coupled with the relentless pounding of the enemy's siege machines, brought about the fall of many castles. Still, some fortresses managed to survive such ordeals. This is partly because many of them had their own artillery pieces in place on the battlements. During the reign of England's Edward I, for example, engineers added four catapults to Chepstow Castle's towers. During sieges at various castles, such catapults, as well as ballistae and trebuchets, had the added advantage of firing from a great height; and they often hurled

THE DREADED GREEK FIRE

One of the most feared weapons in medieval warfare was a combustible product known as Greek Fire. Its exact ingredients are unknown, but it likely consisted of some combination of sulfur, pitch, and other petroleum products, and possibly quicklime. This excerpt from English scholar Christopher Gravett's Medieval Siege Warfare *provides more information about Greek Fire.*

It was probably evolved by the Byzantines in the seventh century, and is likely to have reached Europe via contact with the Crusaders. . . . There were probably several versions in use, based on liquid, paste, and solid mixtures. . . . Greek fire appears to have been difficult to extinguish, water proving useless on its own. The twelfth-century chronicler Geoffrey de Vinsauf, as well as noting the stench, believed that only vinegar could quench it, and that sand could only lesson its ferocity. Though not widely used in the West, it was greatly respected. The Moslems in Acre [in Palestine] hurled jars of the stuff at the Frankish belfries and other structures near the walls and burned everything. The French crusader Joinville vividly describes the roar it made, and the fiery tail . . . it left as it flew through the air.

back the same rocks and spear bolts that the attackers had earlier lobbed into the strongholds.

Castle defenders also regularly exploited the firepower of the crossbow, which had an effective range of between three and four hundred yards. Although besiegers used this weapon too, it was much more effective in the hands of the besieged. The latter had the advantage of firing both from a height and from behind the protection of walls and arrow loops.

On the other hand, some castles avoided capture by exploiting a logistical reality of all warfare, namely the ratio of the amount of food available to the number of mouths to feed. When a castle was extremely well stocked with supplies, ironically the attackers often faced starvation before the defenders. Frances Gies makes the point that some castles kept a year's supply of food or even more on hand, and the relatively small size of a thirteenth-century garrison often meant that in a prolonged siege the assailants rather than the besieged were confronted with a supply problem. A garrison of sixty men could hold out against an attacking force ten times its number, and feeding sixty men from a well-stocked granary supplemented by cattle, pigs, and chickens brought in at the enemy's approach might be far easier than feeding 600 men from a war-ravaged countryside.[37]

Many Variables and Outcomes

Considering these factors, the defenders were often in a stronger position than might be assumed at face value, even when the attacking force was very large. An example of a siege failing in the face of the defenders' superior firepower, ample supplies, and sheer courage and determination occurred in 1216. Louis, dauphin of France, crossed the English Channel and laid siege to Dover Castle (on England's southern coast). Louis's forces encountered such massive and lethal defensive fire that they were forced to move their camp back from its original position. And thanks to the castle's continued strong and heroic resistance, the French finally gave up and lifted the siege.

This and other stories of both successful and unsuccessful sieges teach an important lesson about medieval siege warfare. It was a costly, complex, and uncertain business. And it involved many defensive, offensive, logistical, and human variables that in various combinations could bring about numerous possible outcomes. Some of these outcomes were quite unexpected, both to the participants and to people today.

CHAPTER FIVE

Gunpowder, Cannons, and Handheld Guns

The introduction of guns, including artillery pieces like cannons and handheld pieces constituting primitive rifles, changed the face of medieval warfare. That much is certain. However, the popular idea that gunpowder and guns rapidly rendered castles, trebuchets, crossbows, pikes, and other standard elements of traditional warfare obsolete is a misconception.

In reality, this process was gradual and took several centuries. In the years directly following the introduction of gunpowder into Europe in the early thirteenth century, the substance was not widespread. It was also not very powerful, and it took some time to find the formula that would yield the most explosive effects. Also, early cannons were crude and not very effective against castle and town walls, which were long their main targets. And because they were heavy, immobile, and took a long time to load, they were of little use on the battlefield. Similarly, early handheld guns were at first crude and of limited effectiveness.

It required a steady series of advances, from the early fourteenth through early seventeenth centuries, for both cannons and handheld guns to reach the point where they dominated warfare.

Origins of Gunpowder

The exact origins of the substance that would transform European and world warfare remain unclear. But based on various snippets of evidence, most historians believe that the earliest version of gunpowder was invented in China in the ninth century. Some alert individual noticed that touching a flame to a mixture of charcoal, sulfur, and saltpeter (potassium nitrate) caused an explosive reaction.

Over the course of the following three centuries, the Chinese used gunpowder in firecrackers. They also employed it in various weapons, including "fire lances," bamboo tubes that expelled a burst of smoke and fire when the powder packed inside was ignited. Other weapons were

This illustration, dating from the late 1600s, shows a Venetian army assaulting a Turkish fort. The attackers use cannons and handheld guns, which steadily revolutionized warfare.

called "heaven-shaking thunder," which were grenadelike bombs, and "arrows of fire," small rockets that flew onto and set ablaze rooftops. Evidence also suggests that by the thirteenth century the Chinese were placing gunpowder inside a vase-shaped metal container, perhaps a very early version of a cannon.

Although these developments are impressive, they did not revolutionize Chinese warfare and make China the world's leading military power, which they well might have. First, early Chinese gunpowder produced rather feeble explosions. This was partly because unneeded substances, such as oil, garlic, and honey, were added to the basic ingredients, re-

ducing efficiency. Moreover, as Dunnigan and Nofi point out:

> The proportion of saltpeter is rather low in all Chinese formulas. So these mixtures were far more likely to go off with a "woosh" than a "bang," the more so as we have no way of telling the degree of purity of any of the ingredients. Obviously, impurities would tend to dampen the explosive effects.[38]

Also, Chinese leaders were highly traditional and saw no reason to change the fighting methods employed by their ancestors. So they did not develop and use gunpowder weapons in any systematic or effective manner; and these devices remained largely novelties in China.

Early Gunpowder Weapons

The situation was much different in Europe. Merchants and other travelers brought gunpowder technology from the East to the West sometime in the early 1200s. Various European inventors soon learned of it and began experimenting. In 1267 the English alchemist Roger Bacon introduced a formula that called for 41.2 percent saltpeter, 29.4 percent sulfur, and 29.4 percent charcoal. When ignited, this mixture created an impressive flash and a loud noise. But the explosion produced was weak. Over the next several decades, European experimenters managed to develop versions much closer to the most explosive and destructive formula—74.64 percent saltpeter, 11.85 percent sulfur, and 13.51 percent charcoal.

Added to these developments was the progressive, ambitious, and highly competitive nature of the European kings and nobles. Unlike Chinese leaders, they were willing to try any new idea or device that gave them an edge over their rivals. So

Thirteenth-century English alchemist Roger Bacon conducted important early experiments with gunpowder.

beginning around 1300, they experimented with primitive gunpowder weapons in warfare.

These devices were not guns. Rather, they included handheld grenadelike bombs that attackers catapulted into castles or that defenders dropped onto attackers trying to get inside; barrels of gunpowder that exploded in mines dug under castle walls, in effect the first landmines; and petards. A petard (French for "little fart") was a big metal pot filled with gunpowder. Two or three soldiers carried it to a castle's front door, hurriedly hammered in some nails (while trying to avoid missiles raining down from above), hung the pot on the

Examples of early cannons dating from the mid– to–late fourteenth century. The barrels were made of copper or brass, metals soft enough to cause them to rupture or explode frequently.

STANDARDIZING CANNONS

The cannons of the late Middle Ages came in hundreds of varieties and had numerous names, which people both then and now have found confusing. The reason was that for a long time there was no standardization. Cannons differed widely in design, length, weight, barrel width, firing mechanism, and so forth. Also, Spanish, French, English, German, Italian and other gunmakers often used different measures of length and weight and had their own local names for big guns. Eventually, the need for a more or less standard system of categorizing artillery guns became clear. In the early years of the sixteenth century, most gunmakers adopted such a system based on the weight of cannons and the weight of the balls they fired. In this system, the smallest cannon, often called a falconet, weighed five hundred pounds and fired a ball weighing one pound. A quarter-cannon weighed thirty-five hundred pounds and fired a ball weighing sixteen pounds. And a double-cannon weighed twenty thousand pounds and fired a ball weighing one hundred pounds.

nails, lit the fuse, and ran for cover. If all went well, the explosion knocked down the door. But the petard was only marginally effective, partly because it sometimes exploded prematurely; this is the origin of the phrase, "hoisted by his own petard," indicating someone done in by his own plan backfiring.

The First Guns

These primitive gunpowder weapons continued to be used for centuries. And indeed, the grenade and landmine remain in use today. (The petard was still employed from time to time until the end of the nineteenth century.) But they have relatively little destructive power compared with guns, which quickly eclipsed them in importance in warfare.

The first European guns, crude cannons designed for siege warfare, may have appeared as early as 1320. Later medieval chroniclers mentioned cannons in use at the siege of the independent city of Metz (in northern France) in 1324. The earliest definite reference to such cannons, however, was a 1326 order by the council of the northern Italian city of Florence for the manufacture of a cannon and iron balls. A surviving illustration from that same year shows a vaselike device sitting atop a wooden stand; a soldier has touched off a fuse attached to the weapon, which fires a large dart from its open end toward a castle gate.

At first, these primitive cannons possessed limited military value. They were made of copper or brass, both relatively pliable metals, so they were prone to ripping apart from the force of their explosive discharges. Also, these weapons could not fire their missiles very far and were inaccurate. So they had little effect on the formidable stone fortifications of castles and towns, as evidenced by the description of a cannon attack by the chronicler of the German city of Ulm: "A knight came and besieged the town and shot at it with thunder guns. It did no harm."[39]

The Monster Guns

However, cannon technology rapidly advanced. In the mid-1300s, some gunmakers began casting the tubes from bronze, which is tougher than copper, utilizing methods that had long been used to make large bells for Europe's cathedrals. Another advance came around 1370. Gunmakers started producing larger cannons from long strips of iron. In a process similar to making a barrel from separate strips of wood, they fitted several iron strips edge to edge and held them together by a series of iron hoops that wound around the perimeter. Both the bronze casting and iron composite methods had their advantages and drawbacks. Because a bronze cannon tube was cast as one solid piece, it was less likely to blow apart during firing; but existing casting techniques limited its practical size. And although the risk of rupture was greater in the iron composite tubes, this method allowed

Mons Meg as it appears today at Edinburgh Castle, in Scotland. Originally forged in 1449 by a French duke, the cannon is fifteen feet long and weighs eight and a half tons.

for the construction of much larger cannons. Indeed, in the decades that followed, as iron cannons became larger, they became regular features of siege warfare. By the late 1300s, all such large artillery guns were referred to as bombards (from which the word bombardment derives). At first they fired large stones, similar to those hurled by trebuchets but carefully carved into a ball shape. Over time the stone balls were replaced by lead and iron ones. The gun crew loaded the cannonballs into the muzzle, or open front, of the weapon, hence the term "muzzle-loaded." Loading was no easy task, since an average cannonball weighed between four and five hundred pounds.

It would be an understatement to say that the weapons firing these cannonballs were huge. A bombard made in 1449 by a French duke, which was later given to Scotland's King James II, has survived and is on display in Scotland's Edinburgh Castle. The piece is fifteen feet long, weighs eight and a half tons, and still bears the name its makers gave it—"Mons Meg." In fact, naming large cannons was a common practice in medieval times. Some other known examples include "Great Devil," "Earthquake," "Kill Cow," "Sweet Lips," and "Bumblebee."

With the proliferation of such monster-guns, the lethal effects of cannonfire increased. In 1414, the cannons of a German prince demolished the castle of a rebellious retainer in only two days, an unprecedented event. And in the late 1440s, in the closing stages of the Hundred Years War, French cannons reduced to rubble the English strongholds in northern France with amazing speed. Then came

the even more impressive fall of Christianity's great eastern bastion, Constantinople, to the Ottoman Turks in 1453. In the words of noted scholar John Julius Norwich, the sultan subjected the city's ancient, majestic, and supposedly impregnable walls to:

a bombardment unprecedented in the history of siege warfare. By the evening of the first day he had reduced to rubble a section near the Charisius Gate. . . . The bombardment [continued] uninterruptedly for the next forty-eight days. Although some of the larger pieces [cannons] could be fired only once every two or three hours [because the barrels had to be given time to cool down], the damage they did was enormous; within a week the outer wall across the Lycus had collapsed in several places, and although the defenders worked ceaselessly to repair the damage behind makeshift wooden stockades it was already clear that they could not do so indefinitely.[40]

Lighter, More Mobile Artillery

Despite their firepower, the large bombards had a serious disadvantage that limited their effectiveness in sieges and kept them from becoming useful battlefield weapons. Namely, they were extremely heavy and immobile. Most of the time they rested on heavy, stationary wooden frameworks, or the gun crews dug them into permanent emplacements in mounds of earth. Moving these large cannons to

HOW MANY HORSES TO MOVE A CANNON?

Even the lighter medieval cannons were extremely heavy and required an enormous amount of human and animal power to move from place to place. Through experience, artillery specialists and gunners learned how many horses or oxen and how many wagons would be needed to haul each cannon and its balls, powder, and other supplies and equipment. And various medieval military writers composed manuals listing this information. One such writer, Marc Antonio Bellone, advised that two horses or oxen would be needed to move a small twenty-five hundred pound culverin called a Saker. He said that a larger version, often called a half-cannon, weighing seven thousand pounds, would require seven of these animals. And a large culverin weighing fifteen thousand pounds would need fifteen animals to move it. An artillery train following an army was therefore a huge and cumbersome operation. A relatively small one launched by the Dutch in 1610 to move only fifteen cannons required 700 horses, about 220 wagons, and 16 carts.

their firing positions required considerable time and enormous amounts of labor. According to a fifteenth-century French manuscript, it took twenty-four horses to pull an average-sized bombard through the countryside; and in 1477, two Italian bombards and their cannonballs and gunpowder each required forty-eight wagons. Moreover, such a cannon train moved at a snail's pace and could not keep up with its own army. As a result, renowned military historian John Keegan points out, such large artillery guns

> could be brought into action only on territory their owners already controlled, as the French did the Norman countryside and the Ottomans the water and land approaches to Constantinople. For cannons to become instruments of [military] campaigns they had to be lightened enough to be transported on wheels

at the same speed as the army that accompanied them, so that foot, horse, and guns could move as an integrated unit within enemy territory, thus averting the dangers that artillery might be captured while gunners struggled to keep up with the marching force or have to be abandoned in the event of a retreat.[41]

The obvious solution to these problems was the production of lighter, more mobile cannons. Although the new weapon had many names, the most common was culverin. Its tube, which was cast is a whole piece to make it solid and strong, was longer and narrower than that of a bombard. A culverin was breech loaded by stuffing a portable chamber containing gunpowder, along with an iron cannonball, into the weapon's open rear. The use of such removable firing chambers allowed for much faster reloading than in muzzle-loaded bombards. Culverins were also light enough to make mounting them on mobile two-wheeled carriages practical. After 1450 the technology for such carriages increased rapidly. These improvements made the culverin very movable and flexible; and small versions of it were the first cannons used in open battle.

These technical advances did not happen overnight, however. Many engineering and manufacturing problems had to be overcome before these guns became practical, so development was slow and sporadic. Medieval chronicles are unclear about when and how many of the new cannons were produced and where they were used. A French gunner at the English siege

Wheeled carriages made it practical to carry cannons onto the battlefield. In 1494, France's King Charles VIII made history by fielding a force of forty-four cannons on mobile carriages.

of the French town of Orleans in 1429 may have had a single, primitive culverin. One source suggests that two French culverins broke the English longbow formation in the Battle of Formigny in 1450. And another reports several culverins on two-wheeled carriages in the French town of Rouen in 1454.

The major breakthrough came in 1494. France's King Charles VIII took full advantage of the latest cannon technology available and at great cost ordered the manufacture of four large and forty smaller culverins. All were mounted on two-wheeled mobile carriages, allowing each weapon to be easily maneuvered by a small gun crew. With these weapons in tow, Charles invaded Italy and rapidly demolished the northern Italian castle of Firizzano. Hearing of this event, several nearby Italian city-states promptly

This illustration from a German manuscript dated ca.1400 shows men loading gunpowder into a handheld gun. It originally bore a caption reading in part: "If you want to load your gun professionally, make sure the powder is a good one."

surrendered without a fight. The following year, the fortress of San Giovanni chose instead to defy Charles and paid dearly when his mighty cannon train reduced the place to rubble in a mere eight hours. Charles showed European military leaders that the key to using the new cannons was to concentrate their massed fire on a single, strategic location. John Keegan explains:

The new cannon, because they could be brought rapidly into action close to a wall, and then handled to fire accurately in a predictable arc of impact, transferred the effect of mining [digging saps to undermine the walls] to artillery. Iron cannonballs, directed at the base of a wall in a horizontal pattern of attack that did not vary in height, rapidly cut a channel in the stonework, the cumulative effect of which was to use the physics of the wall against itself. The higher the wall, the more quickly it would become unstable and the wider the breach it left when it toppled. Since in falling it automatically filled up the ditch at its foot with rubble, thus providing passage for an assault party . . . the opening of the breach amounted to the fall of the fortress also.[42]

Handheld Guns

During the same years that cannons were developing, guns that could be carried and fired by a single soldier also made their appearance. They had many names at the time, including hand-bombards, hand-culverins, and handguns. But because they were not

pistols held in one hand, the term handheld gun is used here to differentiate them from modern handguns.

Little is known about the earliest handheld guns, mainly because medieval chroniclers tended to ignore them. The first written descriptions of such weapons date to about 1360; since they refer to devices already in use, these weapons were probably invented two or three decades or more before. Initially, such a gun consisted of a bronze or brass tube between eight and twelve feet long. It was so heavy and awkward that the gunner had to rest it on a pole to fire. According to a German manuscript of about 1390, he poured gunpowder into the muzzle of the barrel, rammed the powder down tight with a stick, then added a small piece of wood and the shot, consisting of a lead ball. To ignite the powder, the gunner inserted a red-hot wire through a small hole bored into the barrel near the breech. An improvement dating to circa 1400 was the "match," a length of smoldering rope that the gunner touched to the hole.

Further advancements in handheld guns were slow but steady. In the early 1400s, the weapon became shorter and lighter so that the gunner could hold it on his shoulder or under his arm when firing. It was still extremely difficult to hold the gun with one hand and ignite the powder with the other, so sometimes a second gunner applied the match. The introduction of the matchlock mechanism in the latter half of the fifteenth century overcame these difficulties. A metal lever bolted to the top of the barrel held the smoldering match in place. When the gunner pulled the trigger, a spring snapped the lever back so that the match touched and ignited a small amount of powder in a tiny pan. The flash then penetrated a hole in the barrel, igniting the powder inside and firing the gun.

By about 1500, a portable matchlock, widely called an arquebus became a common infantry weapon in many parts of Europe. A longer, heavier, and more powerful version, the early musket, also came into use; the gunner usually rested the end of this gun on a forked stick planted firmly in the ground. Generals used groups of gunners as they did units of crossbowmen, mainly to harass an enemy army and soften it up for the attack of the cavalry or infantry phalanx.

The reason it took two centuries for handheld guns to replace crossbows on the battlefield was that the guns had some serious drawbacks. First, they were very slow to load. At best, a gunner could get off only eight to ten shots per hour. Second, these weapons were inaccurate and often unreliable. According to Archer Jones:

Shooting a matchlock remained slow work. . . . While the gunner loaded he had both to keep his match away from the powder and also to keep it alight. This he did af-

ter loading by blowing upon it or by grasping it some distance from the burning end and whirling it around in the air. When ready to shoot, he fixed his match to his hook, opened his pan, took aim, and pulled the trigger. About half of the time the gun shot. . . . The other half of the time his match went out, the powder fell from his pan, the powder flashed in the pan without igniting the charge, or some other accident prevented a shot. If the gun shot, the gunner had about a fifty-fifty chance of hitting a line of men standing shoulder to shoulder about 100 yards away.[43]

Therefore, early handheld guns were no more effective than crossbows in pitched battles. The two main reasons that military leaders adopted these guns was that they were cheaper to make than crossbows and required much less skill and training to use. Since it was more economical to field a force of gunners than an equal force of crossbowmen, handheld guns largely replaced crossbows by the early 1600s. But because they were still not markedly more lethal than crossbows, the guns did not, by themselves, change the outcome of most battles or revolutionize warfare at this time.

CHAPTER SIX

Ships and Naval Warfare

Although often neglected in discussions of medieval warfare, ships played an important role in military campaigns throughout the Middle Ages. Because they moved much faster than land armies, commanders routinely used ships to transport men, horses, supplies, and heavy weapons such as catapults and cannons. Transport vessels could reach a strategic location near or behind enemy lines and unload their contents before the enemy was fully prepared to fight. Or the ships could bring reinforcements or, if necessary, evacuate troops from a dangerous situation.

Ships also directly attacked enemy coasts, disembarking raiders who sacked surprised villages and towns and then safely retreated back to sea. This was the chief tactic of the Vikings, who terrorized the coasts of England and other parts of northern Europe beginning in the eighth century. In describing these onslaughts, a contemporary English chronicler reported:

> Never before has such terror appeared in Britain as we have now suffered from a pagan [non-Christian] race. Nor was it thought possible that such an inroad from the sea could be made. Behold the church of St. Cuthbert, spattered with the blood of the priests of God, despoiled of all its ornaments; a place more venerable than any other in Britain has fallen prey to pagans.[44]

In addition, warships gathered into fleets and engaged in more formal naval battles. Such large-scale encounters were relatively rare, however, because building and maintaining large war fleets was very expensive, and few medieval kingdoms and city-states could

A late thirteenth century painting shows crusaders traveling to the Holy Land aboard a small sailing vessel. The most common military use of ships was as troop transports.

afford it. An average war fleet consisted of no more than fifty ships, paltry compared to some of the huge fleets mounted in the Greco-Roman era. Occasionally, however, the Middle Ages witnessed major sea battles. Two of the largest succeeded in stopping invasions of England across the English Channel: at Sluys, near the northern coast of Flanders, in 1340 (in which England's Edward III defeated the French); and in mid-Channel in 1588 (in which an English fleet defeated the Spanish Armada).

Oared Warships

The medieval centuries witnessed the development of two distinct categories of warships in Europe. The first, which long dominated the waters on both the southern and northern European coasts, was the oared ship. In the Mediterranean Sea, the main type was a galley similar to those used by the ancient Greeks and Romans. A typical medieval galley was a single-masted vessel principally propelled by oars. It was more than a hundred feet long and had one or two banks of oars worked

THE BATTLE OF SLUYS

One of the largest naval battles of medieval times took place in 1340 at the outset of the Hundred Years War between England and France. In preparation for an invasion of England, the French massed about two hundred ships at Sluys, in the mouth of the Zwijn River in northern Flanders. Strengthening these forces were a squadron of warships commanded by a powerful pirate (who joined the enterprise hoping to loot English villages) and more than twenty mercenary galleys from the Italian city-state of Genoa. The English king, Edward III, wisely did not wait for the enemy to come to him. Instead, he led his smaller fleet to Sluys and attacked. About a third of his ships were manned by units of infantry and the rest were loaded with archers. As the English ships approached, the French formed their own vessels into long lines across Sluys's harbor and lashed several of the larger ones together, hoping to create a defensive barrier against the enemy onslaught. But this effort was in vain. Edward made sure to attack when the sun was in the eyes of the French crossbowmen, which greatly reduced their effectiveness. Meanwhile, the English archers found their marks, killing and wounding many French sailors and marines. Then the English marines boarded the enemy vessels and quickly got the upper hand. The final toll was an estimated twenty-four thousand French dead compared with only forty-five hundred English killed.

A late medieval illustration depicts the English naval victory at Sluys in 1340.

by about fifty rowers, although larger versions with a hundred and even two hundred rowers were known. In addition to the rowers, the ship carried a crew of sailors and usually a number of marines (fighters). The large number of people on board gave galleys a significant drawback; namely, there was no room for the supplies needed to feed and maintain them for longer than a few days. So most of the time such ships could not stay at sea very long. Instead, they had to hug the coasts and make frequent stops for supplies, which limited their effectiveness in military campaigns.

The larger rowed warships belonged mainly to Mediterranean kingdoms and city-states with wealth and naval traditions, such as Byzantium (near the southern end of the Black Sea); Venice (on Italy's northeastern coast); and Sicily. However, the peoples of northern Europe also produced warships that used oars in the early Middle Ages. The best known were the Vikings, whose ships were usually smaller than Mediterranean galleys. The largest Viking ship found to date originally measured ninety-two feet long, fifteen feet wide, and had about twenty benches (or forty rowers, since one rower sat on each side of a bench). More common were versions with twelve benches (twenty-four rowers) or fifteen benches (thirty rowers). These were among the vessels the Vikings used to raid the coasts of northern Europe.

Other kinds of oared ships became common as well. The Arabs who inhabited the Near Eastern lands bordering the Mediterranean basin developed a large oared vessel well suited to transporting horses. Called a *tarida*, it was equipped with a stern (rear) ramp. The crew maneuvered the ship toward the shore, then lowered the ramp and unloaded the animals. The Byzantines borrowed the idea and used such vessels extensively during their conquests of the islands of Crete and Cyprus in the tenth century. The French and English also had oared ships. For his invasion of England in 1066, William the Conqueror built a fleet of small oared boats similar to Viking ships. Many of them were equipped with extra platforms running down the middle to ferry horses across the Channel.

A Rapid Series of Advances

These oared ships all had one thing in common: The single square sail with which each was equipped was of limited use. It provided only minimal propulsive power to carry the ship forward, was difficult to maneuver to catch the wind properly, and could not be used at all on windless days. So it often had to be supplemented or totally replaced by the oars.

Beginning in the late thirteenth and early fourteenth centuries, however, a fairly rapid series of important technical advances allowed for the construction of truly practical sailing ships. One innovation was the bowsprit, a wooden spar that projected almost horizontally from the bow (front) of the ship. The crew could now attach the bowlines (running from the mast to the bow) farther forward, allowing the sail to take fuller advantage of the wind.

The added power provided by this advance often caused the ship to keel (turn over or lean) more to one side than the other. This, in turn, created problems with the steering rudders, oarlike devices that projected outward from the rear sides of the vessel. When the ship leaned, the windward rudder lifted too far out of the water and the other one sank too deep into the water to be worked effectively. The solution to these problems was the adoption of a single-stern rudder in the form of a wide strip of wood attached like a vertical hinge to the back of the ship.

These features allowed shipwrights to construct higher, wider hulls, making the vessels sturdier and more stable. Also, there was now a clear difference in shape between the bow and stern (whereas before both ends of a ship had looked the same). The stern grew in height, becoming a "castle." In the old oared ships, castles were makeshift wooden platforms erected on one or both ends of a vessel to provide defensive positions from which to fend off enemy boarders. Now that the hulls of warships could be made higher, the castle was incorporated directly into a ship's structure.

Most important, the new sailing ships, often called roundships, did not need oars. (It must be emphasized that smaller oared vessels, which were cheaper to build and maintain, continued to be used to supplement the larger sailing ships in war fleets throughout the remainder of medieval times.) Eliminating the rowers reduced

Early medieval galleys resembled ancient Roman warships. The main difference between the Norman galley at far left and the Roman ones below is that the Norman version has a single mast.

Roundships had sturdier hulls and could carry more men and equipment than earlier ships. In this medieval illustration, a fleet of roundships prepares to land troops in enemy territory.

the number of men aboard; this factor, combined with the extra interior space provided by the rear castle, created more room for supplies, so that such ships could stay at sea longer. This increased their flexibility in military campaigns, as well as opened the way for explorers to make longer voyages. Merchants benefited as well, since they could make long journeys faster. Of particular note were the excellent merchant fleets turned out in the fourteenth century by the Hanseatic League (a confederation of northern German trading cities).

As a result of these advances, various kingdoms and city-states learned to build roundships. They became increasingly large, partly because larger ships carried more fighters and supplies in wartime. Because it was a symbol of prestige, the flagship of a war fleet, which housed the king or commander, was typically of unusual size and splendor. King Edward's royal flagship at Sluys, the *Thomas*, was ninety feet long, twenty-four feet wide, and displaced (the nautical equivalent of "weighed") 240 tons.

Still another crucial advance was the introduction of the carrack in the early 1400s. This was a sailing ship with more than one mast and consequently multiple sails, for which a complex system of rigging developed. More sails naturally meant increased propulsion and speed, which gave these vessels an important advantage in battle. It also allowed ships to be built even larger than before. The English carrack *Christopher*, built about 1412, was two hundred feet long, fifty feet wide, and displaced fourteen hundred tons.

Naval Battle Tactics

The *Christopher* was also the first known European warship to carry cannons. Along with fourteen other vessels, it was part of the fleet assembled by King Henry V to invade Normandy in 1415. However, each carried only two or three small cannons. And considering how inaccurate and slow-loading such guns were at the time, they could not have made an appreciable impact in a sea battle.

For that reason, the big multimasted warships of the High Middle Ages long relied on the same battle tactics that had been used by roundships and oared vessels for centuries. Essentially, sea battles were fought like land battles. As one warship approached another, archers opened fire (like skirmishers with bows did on land), each side trying to inflict as much damage as possible and soften up the foe. (Fire arrows were used but only rarely

BLINDING THE ENEMY

In addition to the traditional naval tactics of grappling an enemy ship and boarding one's infantry onto it for hand-to-hand fighting, commanders sometimes tried novel, unexpected approaches to disabling enemies. One of the more memorable examples occurred in 1217 in the sea battle of Dover. A mercenary commander, Eustace the Monk, led a formidable fleet of eighty French warships against a force of only thirty-six English vessels under the charge of Sir Hugh de Burgh. The outnumbered English ships took advantage of the wind. First, they maneuvered themselves behind the French fleet and bore down on them, moving with the wind. As his own flagship approached Eustace's flagship, de Burgh had his men toss lime into the wind and then veered away. The wind carried the lime to the French ship, where it blinded the crew and marines. The English commander then moved in and easily captured the disabled vessel.

because of the danger of accidentally setting one's own ship ablaze.)

Eventually, one ship managed to get close enough to toss a grappling hook at the enemy vessel and hold fast. Then, as the archers continued to fire, marines boarded the enemy ship and fought hand to hand. Sometimes a commander ordered several of his ships to be tied together, forming a formidable battle line, as well as a wider platform on which men could fight. The following summary of Viking sea battles of the tenth and eleventh centuries, by English scholar Ian Heath, captures the essentials of European naval tactics through most of the medieval period:

> They made every effort to ensure that a naval action was as much like a land battle as possible, arranging their fleets in lines and

A fleet of Viking raiders crosses from continental Europe to England. These oared vessels were structurally similar to, though smaller than, Mediterranean galleys.

wedges; one side—or sometimes both—customarily roped together the largest of their ships . . . to form large floating platforms. . . . There were usually a number of additional ships positioned on the flanks and in the rear [of the battle line], whose tasks were to skirmish with their opposite numbers; to attack the enemy platform if he had one . . . and to pursue the enemy in flight. . . . The main naval tactic was simply to row against an enemy ship, grapple, and board it, and clear it with hand weapons before moving on to another vessel. . . . Boarding was usually preceded by a shower of arrows and, at closer range, javelins [throwing spears], iron-shod stakes and stones, as a result of which each oarsman was often protected by a second man, who deflected missiles with his shield. . . . Some ships carried extra supplies of stones and other missiles. . . . The largest were dropped from high-sided vessels onto (and even through) the decks of ships which drew alongside to board.[45]

Although such tactics remained the staples of naval warfare, the advent of warships with multiple sails added some new ones. Two obvious advantages such vessels had over oared ships were their ability to take advantage of the wind and their speed. But what happened when one vessel with sails opposed another? In such a situation victory often depended on a combination of favorable wind con-

ditions and the skills and ingenuity of captains and crews. For example, it was difficult for a ship in the leeward position (against the wind) to maneuver well, much less go on the attack. So if possible, the opposing ship tried to place itself in the windward position (with the wind) and strike the enemy before it could swing itself around into the windward. But though such maneuvers were sometimes effective, they were tricky and depended a great deal on the vagaries of the changing winds. So at first they did not play a major role in naval battles, which continued to be dominated by armed boarding parties.

The Advent of Artillery Warfare

A more ideal situation was to combine a sailing ship's speed and ability to utilize the winds with a weapon effective enough to damage or destroy an enemy before it could get close enough to download its marines. The full potential of warships was finally realized in the early sixteenth century, in the closing years of the medieval era. Thanks to various technical advances, these vessels began to arm themselves with powerful cannons mounted in rows below their decks. Equipped with twenty, thirty, or even more large guns, a warship could now produce an artillery barrage capable of crippling any enemy vessel from a distance.

This major development immediately altered naval tactics in two crucial ways. First, it dictated that a captain maneuver his vessel in a broadside-to-broadside array so that his cannons could discharge

87

and rake the enemy ship's hull, masts, and rigging. Second, the advent of massed naval artillery largely spelled the end of infantry combat on ships. (Marines still boarded an enemy, but usually only after it had been badly crippled by cannonfire or had surrendered.)

The major naval campaign signaling the transition to modern artillery warfare at sea was the defeat of the Spanish Armada by the English in 1588. King Philip II of Spain sent about 130 warships, under the command of the Duke of Medina Sidonia, northward into the English Channel. The plan was to help facilitate an invasion of England by troops massed in a Spanish-controlled section of the Netherlands. The Spanish ships were large, most displacing more than five hundred tons. They carried a few cannons, but these guns fired heavy stone balls with relatively short ranges. The shortsighted Philip and Medina Sidonia relied instead on the traditional naval tactic of boarding and fighting hand to hand; to this end, they crammed eighteen to nineteen thousand infantrymen onto the ships, confident that this tactic made them invincible.

The anatomy of a warship. Late medieval naval advances eventually led to warships like this early eighteenth-century English vessel equipped with twenty-eight cannons.

ADVANCES IN NAVAL ARTILLERY

In this excerpt from his History of Warfare, *noted military historian John Keegan explains some of the technical problems that had to be overcome for warships equipped with cannons to rule the waves.*

Since bow-mounted guns could be brought to bear only when the wind was behind, and there was no guarantee that the enemy would appear downwind, any artillery . . . would have to be fired through ports cut in the ship's sides, an arrangement that required both its own . . . technology, in the form of a braking mechanism to absorb recoil, and the devising of a new way of handling ships in battle. With an adaptability akin to that shown by fortress-engineers on land, shipwrights solved the problem almost as soon as it was presented to them. The small fifteenth-century cannons had been housed in "castles" built at bow and stern. When "great guns" were developed at the beginning of the sixteenth century, they were placed below decks, equipped with rope tackle to prevent their careening out of control when discharged, and positioned to fire "broadside." The first ship so constructed is generally held to be the English *Mary Rose*, of 1513; by 1545 an English ship like the *Great Harry* was mounting heavy artillery on two decks; and by 1588 great fleets of ships so equipped fought a running battle up the English Channel lasting seven days [the defeat of the Spanish Armada].

The contrast between the English and Spanish fleets was dramatic. The English commander, Baron Howard of Effingham, a former cavalry officer and seasoned sailor, had more ships—about 190 or so—than his opponent. But they were all smaller than the Spanish warships. Moreover, many of the English ships were merchant vessels hastily pressed into service; and they carried a total of only five thousand soldiers. Considering these disadvantages, Howard was determined not to get involved in a traditional infantry battle. Instead, he planned to outmaneuver the enemy ships and disable them with cannonfire. So he outfitted his fleet with about two thousand cannons, mostly sleek culverins that fired seventeen-pound metal balls and had longer ranges than the Spanish artillery.

In what proved the great showdown between the old and new naval warfare tactics, the English artillery easily won the day. Archer Jones gives this account of one of history's pivotal turning points:

> When the fleets met, the English had the windward position and exploited it when groups of English ships approached the armada in line ahead and, as they passed, fired their broadsides at the Spanish ships. The Spanish ships, which still used the . . . formation characteristic of galley fighting, could make only an inadequate reply. . . . The English secured far more hits and inflicted on the Spaniards losses in personnel and morale. The more maneuverable English ships

The English defeat the Spanish Armada in 1588. Following this great battle and the subsequent voyages of English explorers, England's navy came to dominate the seas.

easily followed Howard's strategy of avoiding Spanish efforts to close and use their boarding tactics and the shock action of their large numbers of fine infantry. . . . As the Spaniards engaged in an artillery duel while moving through the Channel, they had trouble reloading those of their guns mounted on clumsy field artillery carriages. After more than a week of combat, the English . . . realizing the Spanish weakness in firepower, closed the range. Without fear of the Spaniards' boarding their more agile vessels, the English ships came close to the Spaniards and, with the higher velocity of the diminished distance, repeatedly pierced the Spanish ships. During this combat at short range, the Spaniards suffered 600 killed, 800 wounded, and the impairment of the seaworthiness of many of their vessels.[46]

Medina Sidonia eventually saw the futility of his situation and retreated. He led his surviving ships on a torturous homeward voyage around Scotland and Ireland, a fateful trek in which storms destroyed more than half of what remained of his once great armada. The stress of these events caused Medina Sidonia's hair to turn white prematurely. Meanwhile, the English celebrated their deliverance in a chorus of thanksgiving that would echo through the corridors of history. Neither the disappointed Spanish nor proud English had any inkling at the time that they were witnessing the last gasps of what later historians would come to call the Middle Ages.

Notes

Introduction: Medieval Warfare: Romance vs. Reality

1. Clara Winston and Richard Winston, *Daily Life in the Middle Ages.* New York: American Heritage, 1975, p. 48.
2. James F. Dunnigan and Albert A. Nofi, "Just War," *Medieval Life and the Hundred Years War,* 1997, p. 2. www.hyw.com.
3. Nicholas Hooper and Matthew Bennett, *Cambridge Illustrated Atlas of Warfare: The Middle Ages, 768–1487.* New York: Cambridge University Press, 1996, p. 169.
4. Quoted in John Gillingham, *Richard Coeur de Lion: Kingship, Chivalry and War in the Twelfth Century.* London: Hambledon Press, 1994, p. 118.
5. Dunnigan and Nofi, "Logistics," *Medieval Life,* pp. 2–3.
6. Archer Jones, *The Art of War in the Western World.* New York: Oxford University Press, 1987, p. 120.
7. Hooper and Bennett, *Middle Ages,* p. 8.

Chapter 1: Cavalry Weapons and Tactics

8. Bernard S. Bachrach, "Early Medieval Europe," in Kurt Raaflaub and Nathan Rosenstein, eds., *War and Society in the Ancient and Medieval Worlds.* Cambridge: Harvard University Press, 1999, p. 292.
9. Hooper and Bennett, *Middle Ages,* p. 155.
10. Jones, *Art of War,* pp. 151–52.
11. Winston S. Churchill, *The Birth of Britain.* New York: Bantam Books, 1956, pp. 295–98.
12. Thomas F. Arnold, *The Renaissance at War.* London: Cassell, 2001, p. 97.

Chapter 2: Infantry Weapons and Tactics

13. Bachrach, "Early Medieval Europe," in *War and Society in the Ancient and Medieval Worlds*, pp. 286–87.
14. Jones, *Art of War,* pp. 111–12.
15. Dunnigan and Nofi, "Medieval Warfare," *Medieval Life,* p. 4.
16. Dunnigan and Nofi, "Medieval Warfare," *Medieval Life,* p. 4.
17. John Froissart, *The Chronicles of England, France and Spain,* ed. G.C. Macaulay, trans. John Bourchier. New York: Collier, 1910, pp. 102–107.
18. Terence Wise, *Medieval European Armies.* Oxford: Osprey, 2000, p. 24.
19. Douglas Miller, *The Swiss at War: 1300–1500.* Oxford: Osprey, 1999, pp. 13–15.

Chapter 3: Siege Warfare: Castles and Fortifications

20. Joseph Gies and Frances Gies, *Life in a Medieval Castle.* New York: Harper and Row, 1974, p. 187.
21. Christopher Gravett, *Medieval Siege Warfare.* Oxford: Osprey, 2000, p. 3.
22. Quoted in Sidney Toy, *Castles: Their Construction and History.* New York: Dover, 1984, p. 53.
23. John Burke, *Life in the Castle in Medieval England.* New York: Dorset Press, 1992, p. 13.
24. Dunnigan and Nofi, "Sieges," *Medieval Life*, p. 1.
25. Gies and Gies, *Life in a Medieval Castle*, p. 20.
26. Gravett, *Medieval Siege Warfare*, p. 25.

Chapter 4: Siege Warfare: Offensive Weapons and Methods

27. Gies and Gies, *Life in a Medieval Castle*, p. 205.
28. Dunnigan and Nofi, "Medieval Warfare," *Medieval Life*, pp. 6–7.
29. Burke, *Life in the Castle in Medieval England*, p. 75.
30. Burke, *Life in the Castle in Medieval England*, p. 75.
31. Philip Warner, *The Medieval Castle: Life in a Fortress in Peace and War.* London: Barker, 1971, p. 57.
32. Hugh Braun, *An Introduction to English Medieval Architecture.* New York: Praeger, 1968, pp. 212–13.

33. Quoted in Robert Bartlett, *The Making of Europe: Conquest, Colonization and Cultural Change, 950–1350.* Princeton, NJ: Princeton University Press, 1993, p. 74.
34. Quoted in Bartlett, *The Making of Europe,* p. 74.
35. Quoted in Gies and Gies, *Life in a Medieval Castle,* pp. 196–97.
36. Fiona MacDonald and Mark Bergin, *A Medieval Castle.* New York: Peter Bedrick Books, 1990, p. 42.
37. Gies and Gies, *Life in a Medieval Castle,* p. 188.

Chapter 5: Gunpowder, Cannons, and Handheld Guns

38. Dunnigan and Nofi, "Gunpowder," *Medieval Life*, p. 1.
39. Quoted in L. Sprague de Camp, *The Ancient Engineers.* New York: Ballantine Books, 1963, p. 365.
40. John Julius Norwich, *Byzantium: The Decline and Fall.* New York: Knopf, 1996, pp. 423–24.
41. John Keegan, *A History of Warfare.* New York: Random House, 1993, pp. 320–21.
42. Keegan, *History of Warfare,* p 321.
43. Jones, *Art of War*, p. 153.

Chapter 6: Ships and Naval Warfare

44. Quoted in Ian Heath, *The Vikings.* Oxford: Osprey, 2001, p. 3.
45. Heath, *Vikings*, p. 31.
46. Jones, *Art of War*, pp. 211–12.

Glossary

arquebus: The first practical handheld gun used on European battlefields; it was four to six feet long and utilized a matchlock firing mechanism.

arrow loop: (or "murderess"): A narrow vertical slit in a castle wall through which defenders fired arrows and other missiles at attackers.

bailey: A courtyard, usually enclosed by a defensive wall.

ballista: A giant crossbow or spear-thrower.

barbican: An outwork or forward extension of a gate's walls, often forming an outer walled enclosure.

battlement: (or parapet): The top of a defensive wall.

belfry: (or bear): A wooden, wheeled assault tower used to deliver troops and offensive weapons to, and if possible over, a castle's walls.

bombard: A generic name for any large early medieval cannon.

carrack: An early sailing ship with two or more masts.

cat: (also rat, tortoise, or hedgehog): A roofed, wheeled shelter used to protect attacking troops attempting to dig mines, fill in a moat, or operate a battering ram.

coif: A mail hood that covered a soldier's head.

crenellation: The notched effect in the battlements of castles and other medieval structures; the notches are called merlons, and the openings between them crenels.

culverin: A generic name for medieval cannons that were longer, lighter, and more movable than bombards.

drawbridge: A movable wooden platform spanning a moat in front of a castle's main gate; the most common version raised and lowered by means of chains worked by winches in a small chamber over the gate.

fealty: Loyalty.

feudalism: A social system in which freemen provide a noble or other leader with military service in exchange for land tenure.

galley: A single-masted ship propelled mainly by oars; it was used extensively in the Mediterranean Sea in ancient and medieval times.

Gewalthaufen: A phalanx (formation of spearmen) created by the Swiss in the fourteenth century, consisting of twenty rows of foot soldiers wielding eighteen-foot-long pikes.

halberd (or poleax): A long spear with an axlike blade mounted near the end.

hauberk: A mail shirt that stretched to a soldier's knees.

homage: The ceremony in which a retainer swore loyalty to his lord.

keep: (or donjon): The inner, usually highly fortified stronghold of a castle.

lance: A military unit made up of a knight and his retainers and other followers.

levy: In medieval times, a method of conscription in which a king called on all able-bodied men in his realm to serve in a militia for a minimum of forty days.

machicolation: An outward projection of masonry at the top of a defensive wall, the projection containing holes through which defenders dropped stones, fired missiles, and/or poured oil or other liquids.

mail: Rows of iron rings or scales either riveted or sewn together to form a heavy protective shirt.

mangon: A stone-throwing catapult.

manor: An estate held by a lord and farmed by his tenants.

manorial system: The arrangement whereby a lord allowed serfs and other workers to farm portions of his land, in return for which they gave him a share of their harvests and performed various duties and services.

matchlock: A firing mechanism developed about 1450 for handheld guns. When the gunner pulled the trigger, a smoldering piece of rope mounted on the top of the gun made contact with gunpowder in a pan, and the flash ignited the gunpowder inside the weapon, firing it.

motte: An earthen mound on which early castles were built; because most of these had an adjoining lower bailey, they became known as "motte-and-bailey" castles.

musket: In late medieval times, a handheld gun about eight to twelve feet long that utilized a matchlock firing mechanism.

pike: A very long spear.

portcullis: A heavy grated door, usually of oak shod with iron, that raised and lowered vertically in a castle's main gateway.

retainer: (or vassal): In the feudal system, a follower whom a lord granted the use of revenue-producing land (a fief or fee) in return for fealty (loyalty) and military service.

retinue: A group of soldiers supplied by a local lord to fulfill a general citizen levy in wartime.

roundship: An early single-masted sailing ship common across northern Europe in medieval times.

sapper: A miner who dug tunnels (saps) beneath a castle's walls causing them to collapse.

scutage: A tax or fee paid by a retainer to his lord as a substitute for military service.

serf: An agricultural worker tied to a lord's land and bound to serve him for life.

shell keep: A small castle composed of a single circular wall enclosing an inner bailey, usually built atop a hill.

shock action: Direct charges of cavalry units against either cavalry or infantry.

stockade: (or palisade): A fenced enclosure composed of logs or wooden planks set vertically in the ground; for example, the enclosure protecting a motte-and-bailey castle.

surcoat: A loose cloth garment worn by a soldier over his mail suit.

tarida: An oared ship used for transporting horses and supplies in the medieval era.

trebuchet: A large siege machine consisting of a wooden framework that supported a long, balanced beam; the short end of the beam was weighted with a box of stones; the long end, holding a projectile, was pulled down and then released, sending the missile flying in a high arc.

vassal: See **retainer.**

For Further Reading

Timothy Levi Biel, *The Age of Feudalism.* San Diego: Lucent Books, 1994. A broad and easy-to-read overview of the political and social aspects of medieval times, including lords, serfs, vassals, manors, and knights.

Carole Lynn Corbin, *Knights.* New York: Franklin Watts, 1989. A brief, easy-to-read synopsis of medieval knights, castles, and chivalry.

Will Fowler, *Ancient Weapons: The Story of Weaponry and Warfare Through the Ages.* New York: Lorenz Books, 1999. Written for young people, this is an informative and fascinating journey through the history of warfare, including that of medieval times, with hundreds of excellent color drawings and diagrams. Very highly recommended.

Simon Goodenough, *The Renaissance.* London: Latimer House, 1979. A beautifully mounted and illustrated book that explores the main points of the European Renaissance, the last few centuries of the Middle Ages, in which learning, thinking, new inventions, explorations of new lands, and new scientific discoveries all contributed to sweeping changes that heralded the end of medieval society and the beginning of modern times.

Christopher Gravett, *Knight.* New York: Knopf, 1993. Explains what medieval knights wore, their weapons, training, and battle tactics.

Barbara A. Hanawalt, *The Middle Ages: An Illustrated History.* New York: Oxford University Press, 1999. This well-organized and well-written overview of the main historical events of the Middle Ages, aimed at young readers, is also very impressively illustrated. Highly recommended.

Gallimard Jeunesse et al, *Castles.* New York: Scholastic, 1990. Provides the basic facts about medieval castles, including how they were built, their functions, and how they were the focus of siege warfare.

William W. Lace, *The Hundred Years War.* San Diego: Lucent Books, 1994. This easy-to-read summary of the series of conflicts that raged between the English and French from 1337 to 1453 provides a broader context for understanding the political intrigues and bloody struggles that went on during the Middle Ages.

Fiona MacDonald and Mark Bergin, *A Medieval Castle.* New York: Peter Bedrick Books, 1990. A fine, nicely illustrated synopsis of the military functions of, as well as everyday life in, medieval castles.

Neil Morris et al, *Atlas of the Medieval World in Europe.* New York: Peter Bedrick Books, 1999. A useful compendium of facts about Europe in the Middle Ages, with numerous helpful maps and pictures.

Brenda Stalcup, *The 1000s: Headlines in History.* San Diego: Greenhaven Press, 2001. An informative and entertaining overview of important medieval events and developments, written for young adult readers.

Jay Williams, *Life in the Middle Ages.* New York: Random House, 1966. This is a well-written and lively overview of everyday life in medieval times with many colorful illustrations and reproductions of old paintings.

Major Works Consulted

Thomas F. Arnold, *The Renaissance at War.* London: Cassell, 2001. A handsomely illustrated book that surveys warfare in the late Middle Ages, with a strong emphasis on gunpowder and artillery.

Charles Boutell, *Arms and Armor in Antiquity and the Middle Ages.* Conshohocken, PA: Combined Books, 1996. This is a reprint of an old classic written in the 1860s. Although somewhat dated now, it remains useful to scholars.

Hans Delbrück, *Medieval Warfare.* Trans. Walter J. Renfroe Jr., Lincoln: University of Nebraska Press, 1982. One of the classics of the genre, this massive volume begins with the age of Charlemagne and goes on to cover the Normans and Saxons; the Arabs, Turks, and Byzantines; knighthood; mercenaries; archery; sieges; cavalry; and the organization of medieval Swiss phalanxes. A few of Delbrück's arguments are now somewhat dated, but his work remains important overall.

James F. Dunnigan and Albert A. Nofi, *Medieval Life and the Hundred Years War.* www.hyw.com. This is a two-hundred-thousand-word electronic book published in 1997 on the Internet and readily available to everyone. Noted military historians Dunnigan and Nofi have compiled a great deal of information about various aspects of medieval warfare and present it here in a well-organized, well-written work that is accessible and useful to students and general readers.

Christopher Gravett, *Hastings 1066: The Fall of Saxon England.* Oxford: Osprey, 1992. This excellent book covers the invasion of Britain by the Normans, led by William the Conqueror in 1066, in considerable detail, while explaining the weapons, armor, and strategies employed by both sides. An extremely valuable and fascinating book that is also beautifully illustrated.

———, *Medieval Siege Warfare.* Oxford: Osprey, 2000. A very well-written and useful overview of siege warfare in the Middle Ages, supplemented by numerous helpful drawings, paintings, photos, and maps. Highly recommended.

Ian Heath, *The Vikings.* Oxford: Osprey, 2001. Another commendable entry in the Osprey military series, this one examines the Norse warriors who threatened northern Europe and England during the early Middle Ages. Weapons, costumes, fighting methods, and ships are covered in detail.

Nicholas Hooper and Matthew Bennett, *Cambridge Illustrated Atlas of Warfare: The Middle Ages, 768–1487.* New York: Cambridge University Press, 1996. This is one of the better general nonscholarly overviews of medieval warfare, offering both a useful historical sketch of major wars and campaigns and information about weapons and strategies. Also contains an excellent comprehensive bibliography of scholarly books and articles about medieval warfare.

Archer Jones, *The Art of War in the Western World.* New York: Oxford University Press, 1987. An excellent academic, though nonscholarly treatment of the history of Western warfare by a respected military historian.

Jennifer Laing, *Warriors of the Dark Ages.* Gloucestershire: Sutton, 2000. This well-researched volume examines the soldiers and armies of the period of transition between Roman and medieval times, including the Franks, Huns, Vandals, Saxons, Danes, and others.

Douglas Miller, *The Swiss at War: 1300–1500.* Oxford: Osprey, 1999. A fine overview of the all-infantry Swiss armies that reconstituted the ancient Macedonian phalanx during the High Middle Ages. Features stunning color reconstructions of soldiers of the period.

David Nicholas, *The Medieval West, 400–1450: A Preindustrial Civilization.* Homewood, IL: Dorsey Press, 1973. Thoughtfully examines the political, religious, and economic realities of medieval Europe, providing a broader context for studying the warfare of the period.

David Nicolle, *Arms and Armor of the Crusading Era, 1050–1350: Western Europe and the Crusader States.* London: Greenhill Books, 1999. A fulsome, scholarly treatment of weapons and armor in the early High Middle Ages, with hundreds of accurate reconstruction drawings, each accompanied by expert commentary.

———, *The Age of Charlemagne.* Oxford: Osprey, 1999. The soldiers, weapons, armor, and battle tactics of the Frankish armies of the early Middle Ages are examined in this richly illustrated volume.

Kurt Raaflaub and Nathan Rosenstein, eds., *War and Society in the Ancient and Medieval Worlds.* Cambridge: Harvard University Press, 1999. An excellent collection of essays by noted military historians, each summarizing the basic approach to and methods of warfare by an ancient people. The essay on medieval Europe is by Bernard S. Bachrach, of the University of Minnesota at Minneapolis.

Sidney Toy, *Castles: Their Construction and History.* New York: Dover, 1984. One of the best books ever written about castles. It covers the origins of these structures, as well as their construction, defenses, political and economic importance, and ultimate demise. Highly recommended.

Philip Warner, *The Medieval Castle: Life in a Fortress in Peace and War.* London: Barker, 1971. This excellent look at castles during the Middle Ages has excellent descriptions of various aspects of sieges, the central focus of most medieval warfare.

Terence Wise, *Medieval European Armies.* Oxford: Osprey, 2000. A well-written discussion of citizen levies, mercenaries, national armies, movement and supply, the English longbow, Swiss pikemen, and other elements of medieval armies.

Additional Works Consulted

Christopher Allmand, *The Hundred Years War: England and France at War, 1300–c.1450.* New York: Cambridge University Press, 1988.

Charles H. Ashdown, *European Arms and Armor.* New York: Barnes & Noble, 1995.

Kenneth J. Atchity, ed., *The Renaissance Reader.* New York: HarperCollins, 1996.

Robert Bartlett, *The Making of Europe: Conquest, Colonization and Cultural Change, 950–1350.* Princeton, NJ: Princeton University Press, 1993.

H.S. Bennett, *Life in the English Manor: A Study of Peasant Conditions, 1150–1400.* Cambridge: Cambridge University Press, 1960.

M.C. Bishop and J.C. Coulston, *Roman Military Equipment.* Princes Risborough, UK: Shire, 1989.

Hugh Braun, *An Introduction to English Medieval Architecture.* New York, Praeger, 1968.

Peter Brown, *The World of Late Antiquity, A.D. 150–750.* New York: Harcourt Brace, 1971.

John Burke, *Life in the Castle in Medieval England.* New York: Dorset Press, 1992.

Norman F. Cantor, *The Medieval Reader.* New York: HarperCollins, 1994.

——, ed., *The Medieval World: 300–1300.* New York: Macmillan, 1963.

Lionel Casson, *The Ancient Mariners: Seafarers and Sea Fighters of the Mediterranean in Ancient Times.* Princeton, NJ: Princeton University Press, 1991.

Winston S. Churchill, *The Birth of Britain.* New York: Bantam Books, 1956.

William S. Davis, *Life on a Medieval Barony.* New York: Harper and Row, 1951.

L. Sprague de Camp, *The Ancient Engineers.* New York: Ballantine Books, 1963.

Norton Downs, ed., *Basic Documents in Medieval History.* Princeton, NJ: D. Van Nostrand, 1959.

Zoroslava Drobná and Jan Durdík, *Medieval Costume, Armor, and Weapons.* Trans. Eduard Wagner. Mineola, NY: Dover, 2000.

Arther Ferrill, *The Fall of the Roman Empire: The Military Explanation.* New York: Thames and Hudson, 1986.

Anne Fremantle, *Age of Faith.* New York: Time, 1965.

John Froissart, *The Chronicles of England, France and Spain.* Ed. G.C. Macaulay. Trans. John Bourchier. New York: Collier, 1910.

Joseph Gies and Frances Gies, *Life in a Medieval Castle.* New York: Harper and Row, 1974.

———, *Life in a Medieval City.* New York: Harper and Row, 1969.

John Gillingham, *Richard Coeur de Lion: Kingship, Chivalry and War in the Twelfth Century.* London: Hambledon Press, 1994.

V.H.H. Green, *Medieval Civilization in Western Europe.* New York: St. Martin's Press, 1971.

Sir John Hackett, ed., *Warfare in the Ancient World.* New York: Facts On File, 1989.

George Holmes, ed., *The Oxford History of Medieval Europe.* New York: Oxford University Press, 1989.

John Keegan, *A History of Warfare.* New York: Random House, 1993.

Simon Macdowall, *Late Roman Infantrymen, 236–565 A.D.* London: Osprey, 1994.

E.W. Marsden, *Greek and Roman Artillery.* Oxford: Clarendon Press, 1969.

John Julius Norwich, *Byzantium: The Decline and Fall.* New York: Knopf, 1996.

Colin Platt, *The Castles of Medieval England and Wales.* New York: Barnes & Noble, 1996.

Justine Davis Randers-Pehrson, *Barbarians and Romans: The Birth Struggle of Europe, A.D. 400–700.* Norman: University of Oklahoma Press, 1983.

James B. Ross and Mary M. McLaughlin, eds., *The Portable Medieval Reader.* New York: Viking Press, 1972.

R.C. Smail, *Crusading Warfare, 1097–1193.* New York: Cambridge University Press, 1977.

Pat Southern and Karen R. Dixon, *The Late Roman Army.* New Haven, CT: Yale University Press, 1996.

Hans Talhoffer, *Medieval Combat.* Trans. and ed. Mark Rector. London: Greenhill Books, 2000.

Brian Tierney, ed., *The Middle Ages, Volume I: Sources of Medieval History.* New York: Knopf, 1970.

———, ed., *The Middle Ages, Volume II: Readings in Medieval History.* New York: Knopf, 1970.

F.W. Walbank, *The Awful Revolution: The Decline of the Roman Empire in the West.* Toronto: University of Toronto Press, 1969.

John Warry, *Warfare in the Classical World.* Norman: University of Oklahoma Press, 1995.

Eugen Weber, ed., *The Western Tradition: From the Ancient World to Louis XIV.* Boston: D.C. Heath, 1965.

Lynn White Jr., *Medieval Technology and Social Change.* London: Oxford University Press, 1962.

Clara Winston and Richard Winston, *Daily Life in the Middle Ages.* New York: American Heritage, 1975.

Index

Picture Credits

Cover Photo: © Archivo Iconografico/ CORBIS
© Paul Almasy/CORBIS, 48
© Arhivo Iconografico, S.A./CORBIS, 19, 84
© Bettmann/CORBIS, 35, 56, 61, 72, 80
© Christie's Images/CORBIS, 11
Dover Publications, Inc., 20, 23, 29, 31 (both), 39, 49, 52 (both), 59, 82, 83, 88

© Mary Evans Picture Library, 86
© Christel Gerstenberg/CORBIS, 76
© Historical Picture Archive/CORBIS, 68
© Hulton Archive, 45, 69, 70, 75, 90
Library of Congress, 25, 36, 38, 43, 63, 81
© Buddy Mays/CORBIS, 57
© North Wind Picture Archives, 12, 14, 17, 22, 33, 42, 50 (both)

About the Author

Historian Don Nardo has written numerous volumes about the ancient and medieval worlds, among them *The Assyrian Empire, Games of Ancient Rome, Greek and Roman Science, The Decline and Fall of the Roman Empire, Life on a Medieval Pilgrimage*, and *The Black Death.* Mr. Nardo resides with his wife, Christine, in Massachusetts.